FURNITURE
FROM THE HISPANIC
SOUTHWEST

EDITED BY

WILLIAM WROTH

ANCIENT CITY PRESS
SANTA FE, NEW MEXICO

© Copyright 1984 by Ancient City Press, Inc.
P.O. Box 5401
Santa Fe, New Mexico 87502

Library of Congress Catalogue Number
84-071137
International Standard Book Number
0-941270-18-1

Third Printing

Designed by Mary Powell

Cover design by Stephen Tongier

Printed in the United States of America
by Inter-Collegiate Press
Shawnee Mission, Kansas

CONTENTS

PREFACE

In 1933 the New Mexico State Department of Vocational Education (SDVE) launched an ambitious training program to teach traditional Spanish crafts in towns and villages across northern New Mexico. Brice H. Sewell, State Supervisor of Trade and Industrial Education, directed this project, which was designed to combat the devastating economic effects of drought and depression on the area's Hispanic communities. Vocational schools at Taos and Penasco in Taos County and at Chupadero, La Cienega and Galisteo in Santa Fe County were among the earliest established. By utilizing the resources of several state and federal government agencies Sewell was able to expand the program so that by 1936 nearly every Hispanic community of any size had its own vocational school. They ranged from those offering one or two classes in a small rented storefront to full-fledged centers such as the Taos Vocational School with its own adobe building constructed by the local community.

The vocational schools' curriculum centered around weaving, tanning and leatherwork, furniture-making and ornamental ironwork. To insure that teachers and students adhered to authentic New Mexican designs and types of pieces, a series of **Trade and Industrial Bulletins** was published during the 1930s and distributed to all the schools. These **Bulletins** were edited by SDVE staff member Carmen Espinosa in Santa Fe. She carefully researched their content and supervised their precise, attractive drawings, some of which she drew, of genuine Spanish Colonial pieces.

The SDVE had limited resources, and the Spanish crafts **Bulletins** had to be rather crudely printed by mimeograph on cheap paper. Nevertheless, they were highly prized by both the vocational teachers and their students. Some, like the **Spanish Colonial Furniture** and the **New Mexico Colonial Embroidery Bulletins**, went through several editions and continued in use through the 1940s.

Brice Sewell envisoned the village vocational schools not merely as educational institutions but as centers for the revitalization of communities—means by which villagers could regain control of their own destinies through learning economically viable trades based upon their traditional resources. Indeed, the new schools were greeted enthusiastically by those eager to make a living during perilous economic times. With the onset of the Depression outside sources of employment had quickly evaporated, bringing men back home with no source of income, and in many areas large numbers of families were forced to go on relief. The vocational schools helped revive old hand skills, and many families were able to get off relief rolls by selling their handicrafts.

The success of Sewell's program depended in large part on the aesthetic appreciation of Hispanic crafts fostered during the 1920s by Santa Fe artists and patrons. A small but determined group of individuals headed by writer Mary Austin and artist Frank Applegate were responsible for rediscovering the village crafts. In 1925 they started the Spanish Colonial Arts Society in Santa Fe with the express purposes of saving and documenting craft traditions then on the verge of dying out and of encouraging talented villagers to take up the handwork of their forebears. During the late 1920s the society established the Spanish Market to display and sell crafts during the annual Santa Fe Fiesta and between 1930 and 1933 sponsored The Spanish Arts shop in the Sena Plaza as a year round crafts outlet. These volunteer efforts by an enthusiastic group of Santa Fe patrons began a revival of interest in and a market for traditional forms of handwork such as weaving, colcha embroidery, furniture-making, wood carving and tinwork.

Like the Spanish Colonial Arts Society members, Brice Sewell was well aware that for handicrafts to compete with machine-made products they had to be superior both in authenticity of design and quality of construction. In the **Trade and Industial News** of March 1936 (vol. 2, no. 2), he claimed that "for the handmade products to be saleable, the students must be thoroughly grounded in the knowledge of the best examples of the past, particularly the Spanish Colonial, and the finished article must be superior in beauty and durability to the machine-made product." He was satisfied that in many cases these criteria had been met and that "the students who have mastered the trade are now practically all employed as wage earners in the trade, or are self-employed and are making their livelihood through the sale of their products."

Because of their historic and artistic significance, the more important SDVE crafts **Bulletins** are being reprinted by Ancient City Press in a more permanent and usable form. The original title pages and forewords have been typeset, as have all titles and notes on the original mimeographs. Mary Powell of Ancient City Press has painstakingly traced the old mimeographed drawings. Her skill as a designer has made it possible to present an accurate rendering of the important 1930s work of William Lumpkins, Carmen Espinosa, Brice H. Sewell and others.

Selected References:

Boyd, E. **Popular Arts of Spanish New Mexico.** Santa Fe: Museum of New Mexico Press, 1974.

Dickey, Roland F. **New Mexico Village Arts.** Albuquerque: University of New Mexico Press, 1949.

Nestor, Sarah. **The Native Market of the Spanish New Mexican Craftsmen: Santa Fe, 1933-1940.** Santa Fe: Colonial New Mexico Historical Foundation, 1971.

Weigle, Marta. "The First Twenty-Five Years of the Spanish Colonial Arts Society." In **Hispanic Arts and Ethnohistory in the Southwest**, ed. Weigle with Claudia Larcombe and Samuel Larcombe, pp. 181-203. Santa Fe: Ancient City Press; Albuquerque: University of New Mexico Press, 1983.

Wroth, William. "Introduction: Hispanic Southwestern Craft Traditions in the 20th Century." In **Hispanic Crafts of the Southwest**, ed. Wroth, pp. 1-7. Colorado Springs: The Taylor Museum of the Colorado Springs Fine Arts Center, 1977.

Wroth, William. "New Hope in Hard Times: Hispanic Crafts Are Revived During Troubled Years." **El Palacio** 89, 2 (Summer 1983): 22-31.

FURNITURE-MAKING IN NEW MEXICO

Furniture-making was one of the most important crafts in Colonial New Mexico. From the first Spanish colony in 1598 through the mid-nineteenth century, settlers had to rely on local craftsmen because of great difficulties in importing large, bulky pieces. Working with native pine wood and simple hand tools they produced all the necessary pieces for homes and churches—chairs and tables, dish cabinets, wardrobes, shelves, chests, doors, altars and altar screens.

In New Mexico all the crafts were quite unaffected by the more complicated Baroque design tendencies of artisans in the urban centers of Spain and Mexico. Simple, elegant furniture was built in the colony by local artisans who reproduced types of pieces dating back to Spain's Middle Ages and decorated them with carved and painted designs of even greater antiquity. Popular New Mexican designs such as the rosette or spoked wheel motif and the opposed lion motif may be traced back to the pre-Christian ancient Near East, from where they later diffused throughout Europe. These motifs were preserved into recent centuries by folk artists in both the Old and New Worlds, and they survived in New Mexico well into the nineteenth century.

After the American occupation of New Mexico in 1846, eastern Anglo-American furniture was imported, and new and better tools such as saws and planes became available to the Hispanic furniture-makers. For a brief period there was a flowering of more elaborate pieces and new decorative motifs. Delicate cut-out designs were more easily made, and the furniture produced often reflected the influence of eastern and even European styles. This uniquely New Mexican Territorial furniture style had its counterpart in the Territorial architectural style of the period with its adaptation of eastern forms.

By 1900 this brief flowering of a New Mexican Territorial furniture style had for all practical purposes ended. New Mexicans of all races were increasingly dependent upon expensive imported furniture and for some twenty years indigenous furniture-making was all but forgotten. The first interest in a revival of Hispanic furniture came in 1917. Museum of New Mexico staff members Kenneth Chapman and Jesse Nusbaum were furnishing Santa Fe's new Fine Arts Museum and drew upon colonial New Mexican prototypes which they "found in out-of-the-way places in New Mexico where woodcarvers and craftsmen in the early days fashioned the furniture and embellishments of the home" (**El Palacio**, vol. 7, no. 4, 1919, p. 89).

In the 1920s furniture-making was vigorously promoted by the Spanish Colonial Arts Society and later became the most important and economically viable craft of the SDVE programs. Commissions for furnishing public buildings all over the state as well as private commissions were given to the vocational schools and thousands of pieces were made. The high quality and consistency of design in this work, much of it done by students under the direction of a teacher, seems quite remarkable today. To a large degree it can be attributed to the carefully researched **Bulletins** of the SDVE which are reproduced in this publication.

Beginning with the **Spanish Colonial Furniture Bulletin** of October 1933, the SDVE issued a series of measured drawings depicting the authentic old pieces of furniture. The **Furniture Bulletin** was for the most part the work of

William Lumpkins. As a teacher in the vocational program he was assigned to the isolated northern mountain village of Penasco. While there he recorded fine examples of colonial furniture still in daily use by the residents and made careful measured drawings of all cupboards, chairs, chests, doors and other pieces. Lumpkins' work in the Penasco area was supplemented by drawings of pieces in museum and private collections, notably the excellent collection of Frank Applegate, one of the founders of the Spanish Colonial Arts Society in Santa Fe.

The lucid foreword to the **Spanish Colonial Furniture Bulletin**, probably written by Brice H. Sewell, gives useful background information and clearly distinguishes true New Mexican colonial work from "the so-called Spanish Mission Style of furniture which was recently in vogue and [is] so displeasing because of its illogical massive qualities and monotonous design." The **Furniture Bulletin** was followed by **New Adaptations from Authentic Examples of Spanish Colonial Furniture** (n.d.), **Graphic Standards for Furniture Designers** (1939, not reproduced here), and **Spanish Colonial Painted Chests** (1937), for which Carmen Espinosa wrote the introduction. The last mentioned was the first publication on the subject of painted chests. In her introduction to this **Bulletin** Espinosa raised the question of whether or not the gaily painted chests were made in New Mexico or imported from Mexico, an issue still hotly debated by Spanish Colonial specialists today.

These furniture **Bulletins** are of immense value to today's furniture-makers who wish to reproduce authentic Hispanic pieces. The drawings provide enough detail for the worker to reproduce pieces exactly or else to make creative adaptations utilizing the design motifs, types of pieces, and even old joining methods. Short of having the original pieces in hand to work from, there is no other comparable source available today for the real New Mexican colonial furniture.

Selected References (in addition to those above):

Taylor, Lonn. "New Mexican Chests: A Comparative Look." **El Palacio** 89, 2 (Summer 1983): 32-41.

Taylor, Lonn, and Dessa Bokides, curators. **Carpinteros and Cabinetmakers: Furniture Making in New Mexico, 1600-1900**. Santa Fe: Museum of International Folk Art, Museum of New Mexico, 1983.

Vedder, Alan C. **Furniture of Spanish New Mexico**. Santa Fe, New Mexico: Sunstone Press, 1977.

Vedder, Alan C. "Spanish New Mexican Furniture: Past and Present." In **Hispanic Crafts of the Southwest**, ed. William Wroth, pp. 27-35. Colorado Springs: The Taylor Museum of the Colorado Springs Fine Arts Center, 1977.

SPANISH COLONIAL FURNITURE

This collection of drawings has been compiled that authentic information regarding the old Spanish Colonial furniture may be available to the modern cabinet maker; also, to give reliable information to the buying public as to design and types of furniture that were formerly produced in the Southwest. This type of furniture, with proper adaptations, is particularly well suited to the Southwestern type of architecture that has been revived and is prevalent in this region. The furniture is contemporary with this period of architecture.

It is necessary for both the craftsman and the home owner to know some of the important points about authentic old examples. The first principle of good furniture and one rule that has been conformed to throughout the ages is that the shape and style of the furniture be governed by the use to which the furniture is to be placed. This also holds true of any part or section of any piece of furniture. For example, the first function of the arm of the chair is to support at a restful height or angle the arm of the person sitting in the chair; the back of the chair should support and rest the back of the occupant. If it does not do this comfortably, it is not serving its purpose. Hence, the slant and height of the back of the chair is governed by comfort. A chair used for state occasions and formal functions must necessarily be designed in a more upright position, as the occupant would wish to sit in a dignified posture. In this type there are admirable examples of Spanish Colonial furniture.

The second principle is that the furniture must be pleasing to the eye as well as serviceable and comfortable, but a great deal of this beauty must be achieved through pleasing proportions. There must never be more carving used as a decoration than is absolutely necessary to relieve the monotony of some plain surface. Carving is used where it will not interfere with the usability or serviceability of that particular member or part of the piece of furniture. Chests were rarely carved as the carving would interfere with comfort when sometimes they were used as seats. Tops of tables, of course, were never decorated with carving nor were the arms of chairs, and when carving was used on the backs of chairs, it was always incised instead of raised so that it might not interfere with the comfort of the person using the chair.

The third principle is that the craftsman adapt his technique to the material at hand. In this, also, we can learn an important lesson from the woodworker of Spanish Colonial times. In Spain and Old Mexico the woodworkers had an abundance of hard wood which when well-seasoned is admirably suited for cabinet making.

The ordinary concealed joint similar to the type of joint used in most of our manufactured furniture formed a sufficient bond in the construction. However, when the craftsman of that period arrived in New Mexico he found only a soft native pine wood available which was very difficult to season and had a tendency to warp and shrink even after it was worked up into furniture, particularly so in the arid climate of the Southwest. It was to meet these conditions that the full mortise and tenon joint came into universal use, as in this type of joinery wooden wedges could be inserted in any wooden furniture to take up any play that might be developed.

The tenon of the joint was never allowed to protrude from the mortise but was cut off flush with the surface and well-smoothed. As soft pine is still the most readily available and economical wood, it is necessary for our modern cabinet workers to use this same type of joinery. Also, it should be noted that square or hexagon wooden pegs were used in preference to the round peg as it could be driven in more tightly without danger of splitting the surface and surrounding wood. Nails and screws were never used, not because of the difficulty in securing them, but because introducing a foreign material into the wood does not make for permanent construction. It should be noted that in the better classes of manufactured furniture today, very few nails, screws, or steel plates are used.

We find rounded edges in place of sharp edges in most of the old pine furniture, for if the edge were left sharp, as is commonly done in hard wood, there was danger of splintering the wood when subjected to hard usage; therefore, the cabinet maker removed this danger by rounding the edges when he constructed the furniture. Incidentally, this rounded effect harmonizes well with the soft round edges of the adobe plaster which was used in architecture for the same reason. The Spanish Colonial furniture made in New Mexico carried the traditional designs prevalent in medieval Spain at that time; although they were somewhat simplified particularly in regard to the carving so that they might be adapted to soft wood in which intricate design is not practical.

A strong Moorish influence may be noted particularly where spindles are used. There was never in the medieval furniture, nor in the furniture of Spanish Colonial New Mexico an excess of carving. Just enough decoration was used to break the monotony of the plain surface. The ornate type of carvings that are found in Old Mexico and Spain today are an outgrowth of the Italian Renaissance which became what is known as the "rococo style" in Spain and was used to some extent in the Spanish Colonial period in California. New Mexico escaped practically all of this influence due to the fact that New Mexico was settled by Spanish people of the Interior who left for colonies in the New World. After the first few waves of colonization, contact with the mother country became less when they found that the country was poorer in natural resources than they had expected. For centuries the colonies here remained practically isolated even from the cultural centers of Old Mexico. The journey was long and hazardous, and as a result we have preserved even up the present time a great deal of the medieval culture of Old Spain.

In the making of modern furniture, it is suggested that the woodworker adapt the best qualities of the old traditional designs, paying particular attention to modern needs particularly in regard to proportions and comfort, but great care should be taken to keep the feeling of simplicity and honesty of construction that is found in the original pieces.

There is a tendency for the hand craftsman to make his furniture too heavy and cumbersome. While pine wood naturally requires somewhat heavier construction than hard wood, it should never be heavier than is necessary for the strain that the particular piece or section of furniture is to be subjected.

It should be noted from the above information that there is very little relationship between true Spanish Colonial furniture and the so-called Spanish Mission Style of furniture which was recently in vogue and so displeasing because of its illogical massive qualities and monotonous design.

Front elevation

End elevation

TRASTERO FROM APPLEGATE COLLECTION

Scale 1/8"=1"

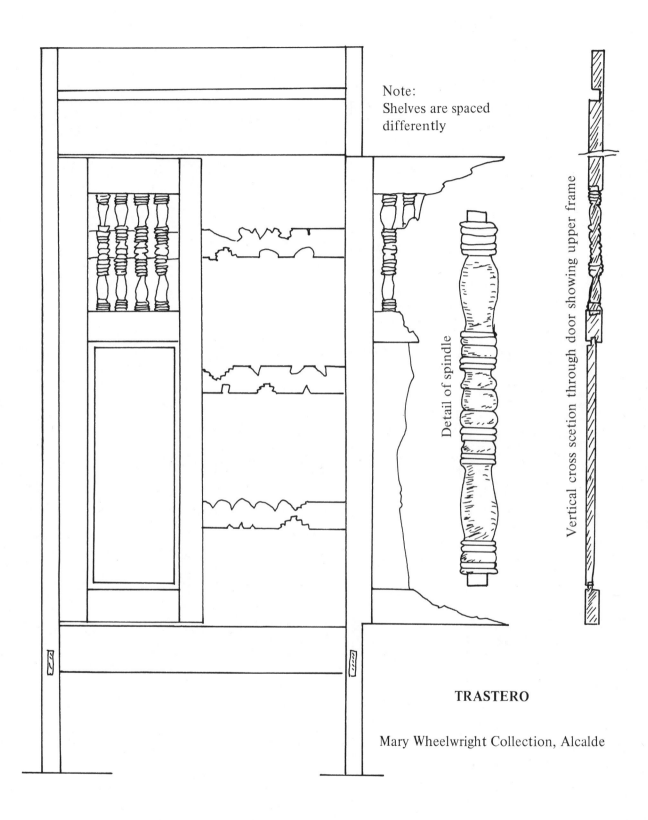

Note:
Shelves are spaced differently

Detail of spindle

Vertical cross scetion through door showing upper frame

TRASTERO

Mary Wheelwright Collection, Alcalde

Detail of upper bracket

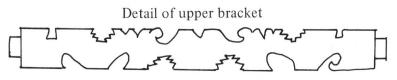

End view

Door is restored

Front view

Scale 1/8" = 1"

PAINTED TRASTERO FROM APPLEGATE COLLECTION

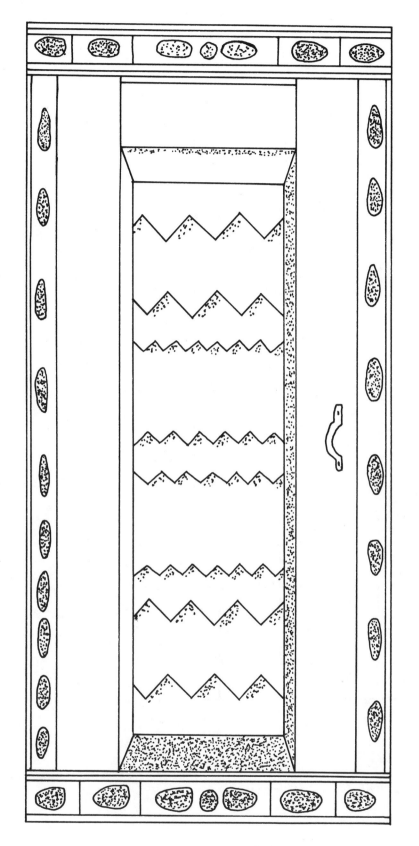

Vertical cross-section
through center - showing
also upper trim

Pin at top and bottom
used as hinge

DOOR TO TRASTERO

Field Collection

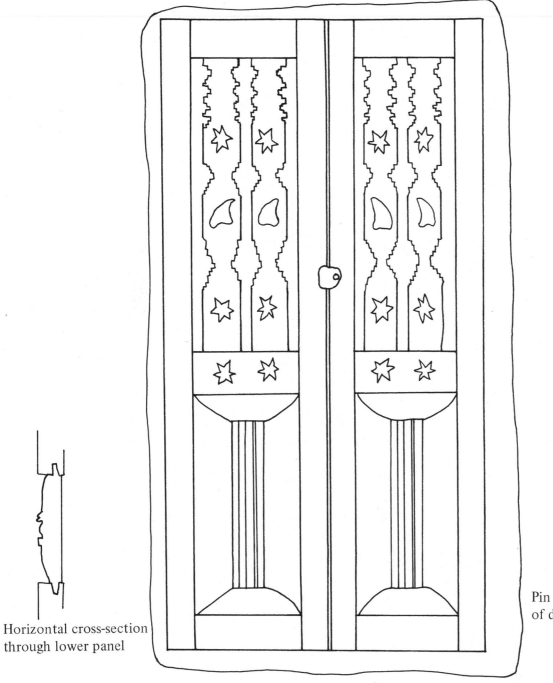

Horizontal cross-section
through lower panel

Pin in four corner
of door in place of hinge

DOOR TO TRASTERO

Mary Wheelwright Collection, Alcalde

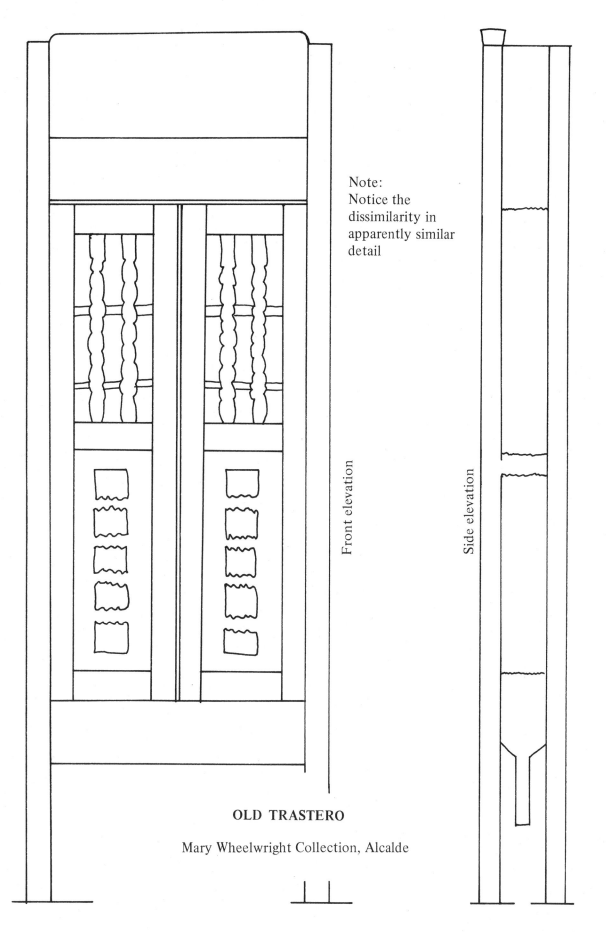

Note:
Notice the
dissimilarity in
apparently similar
detail

Front elevation

Side elevation

OLD TRASTERO

Mary Wheelwright Collection, Alcalde

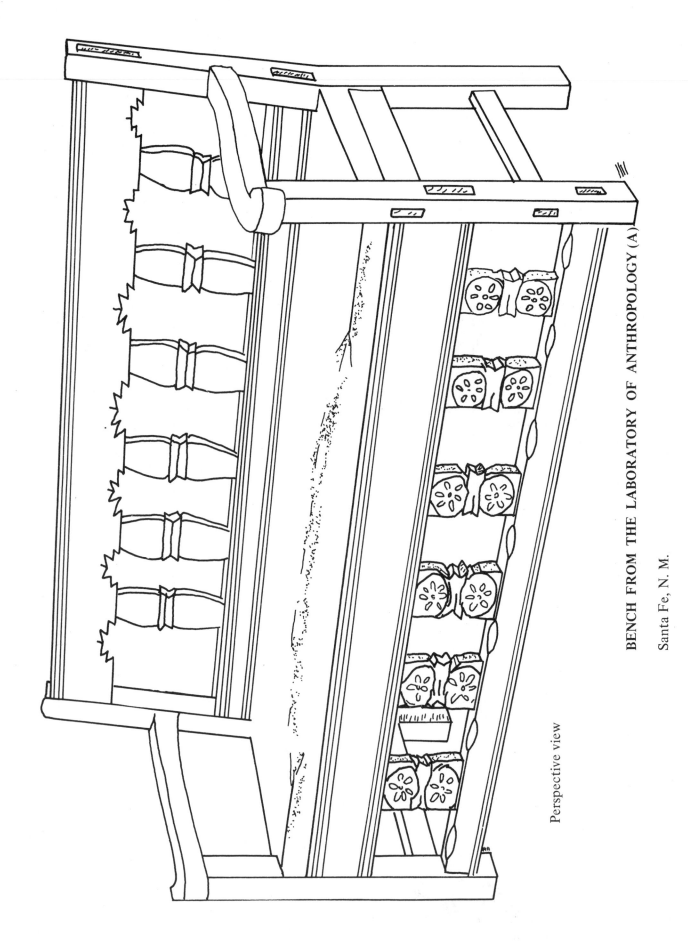

BENCH FROM THE LABORATORY OF ANTHROPOLOGY (A)

Santa Fe, N. M.

Perspective view

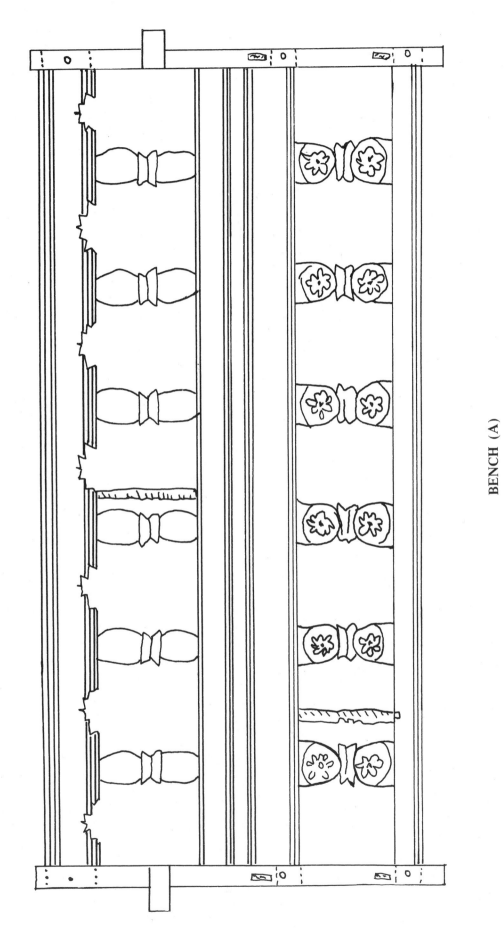

BENCH (A)

Front elevation
Scale 1/8" = 1"

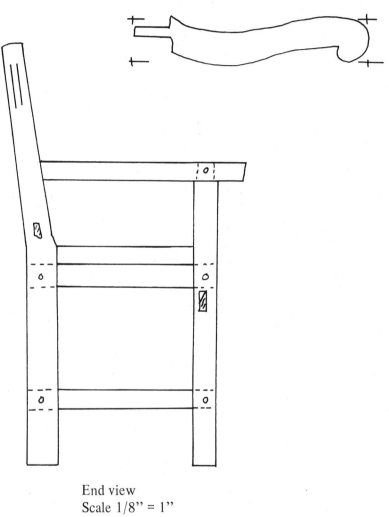

End view
Scale 1/8" = 1"

BENCH (A)

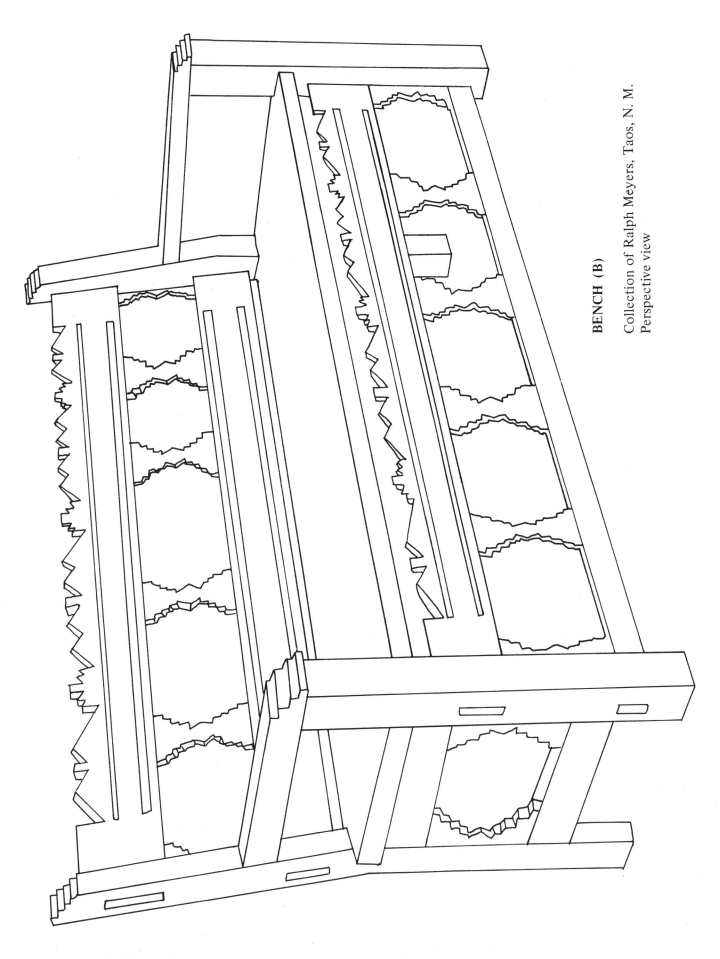

BENCH (B)

Collection of Ralph Meyers, Taos, N. M.
Perspective view

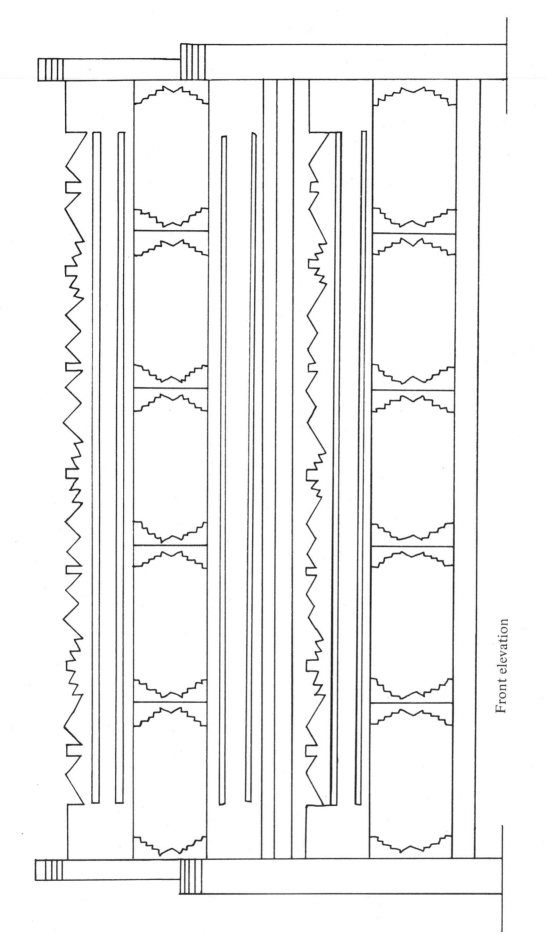

BENCH (B)
Collection of Ralph Meyers, Taos, N. M.

Front elevation

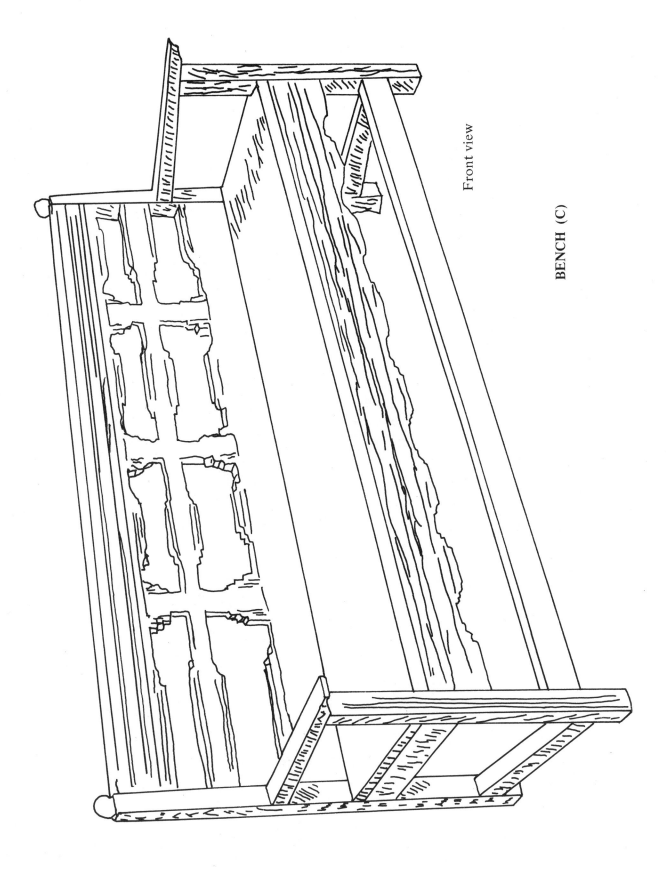

Front view

BENCH (C)

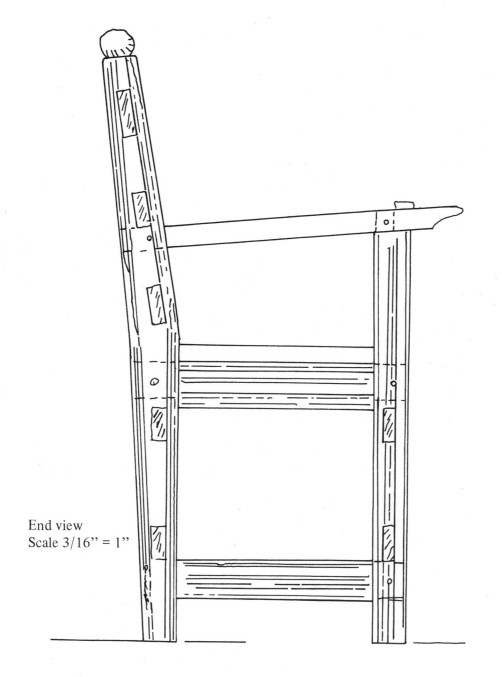

End view
Scale 3/16" = 1"

BENCH (C)

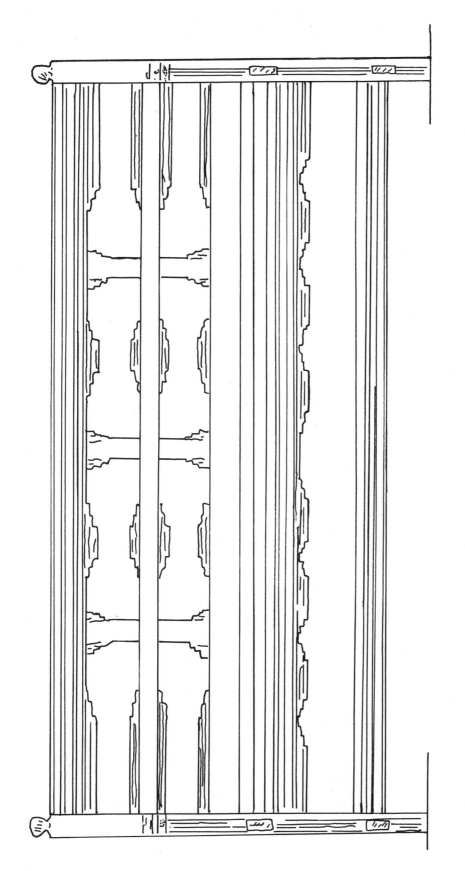

BENCH (C)

Front view

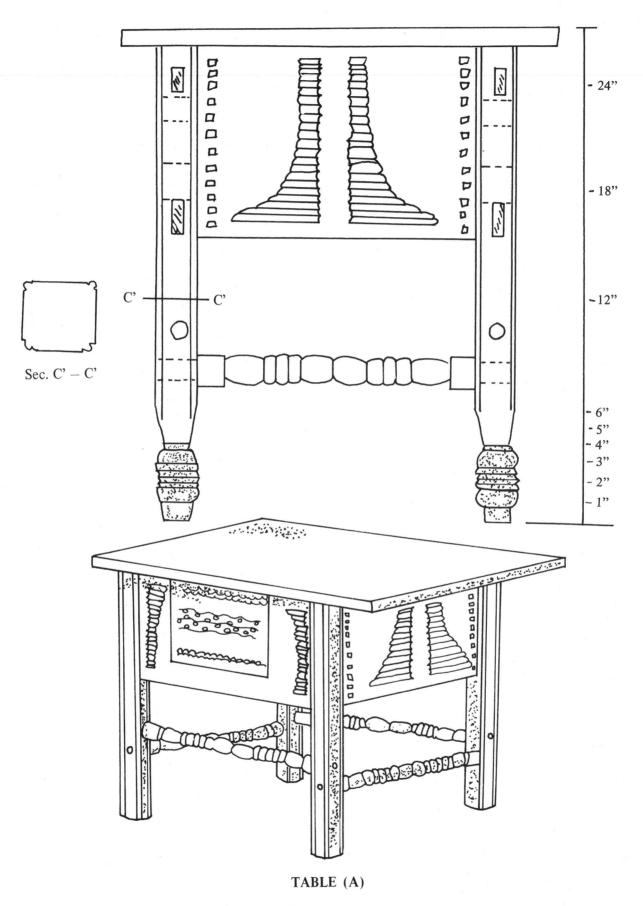

Sec. C' — C'

TABLE (A)

Penasco area

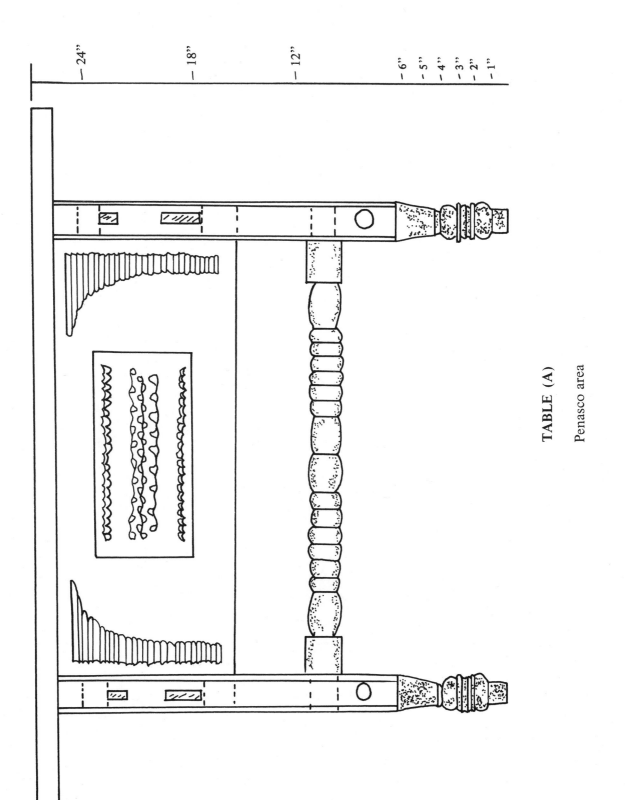

TABLE (A)

Penasco area

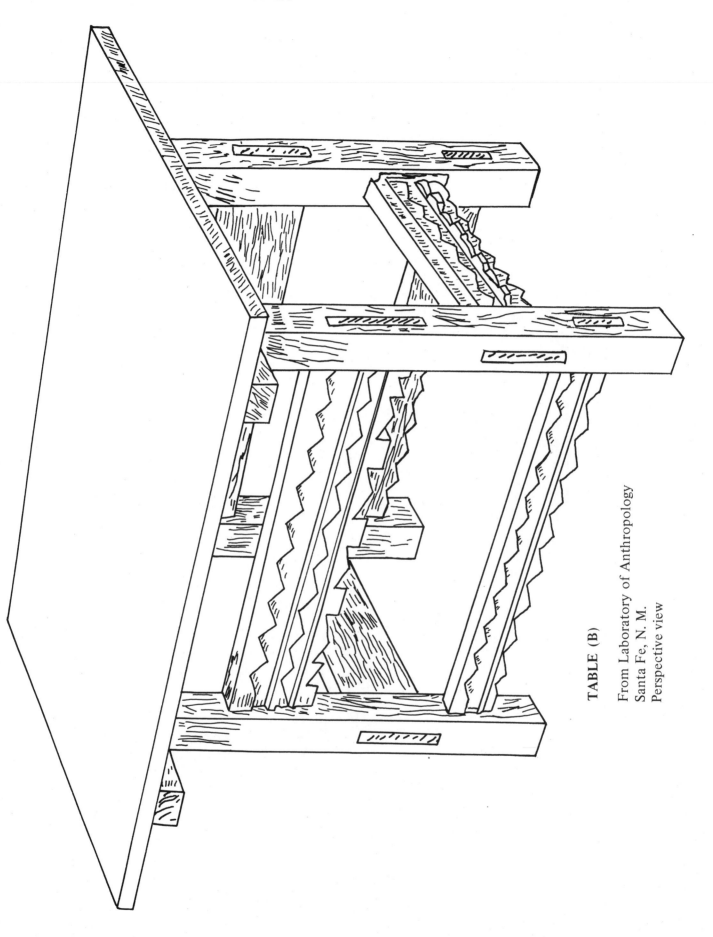

TABLE (B)

From Laboratory of Anthropology
Santa Fe, N. M.
Perspective view

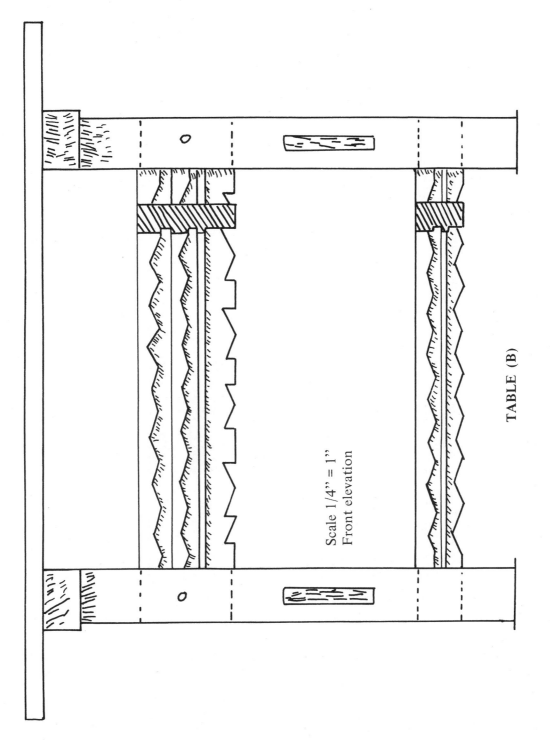

Scale 1/4" = 1"
Front elevation

TABLE (B)

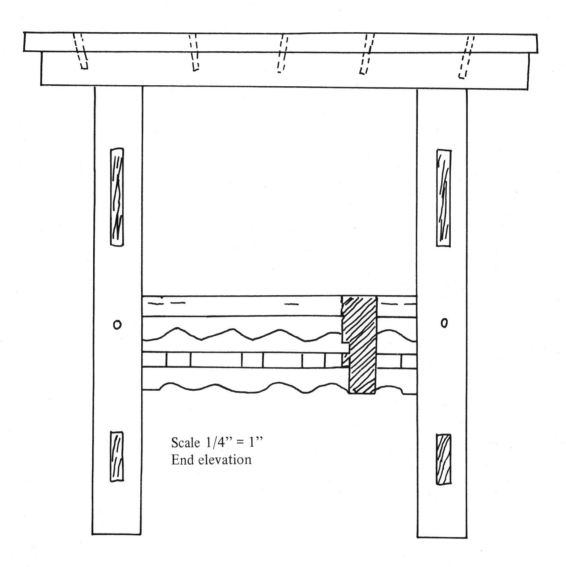

Scale 1/4" = 1"
End elevation

TABLE (B)

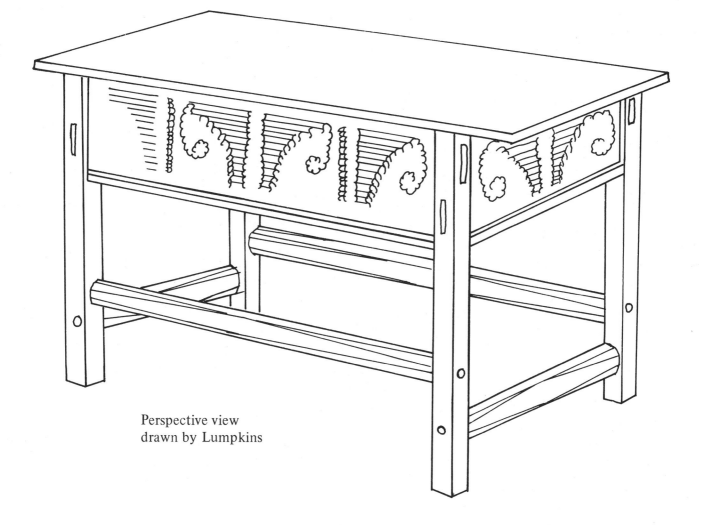

Perspective view
drawn by Lumpkins

TABLE - PENASCO AREA (C)

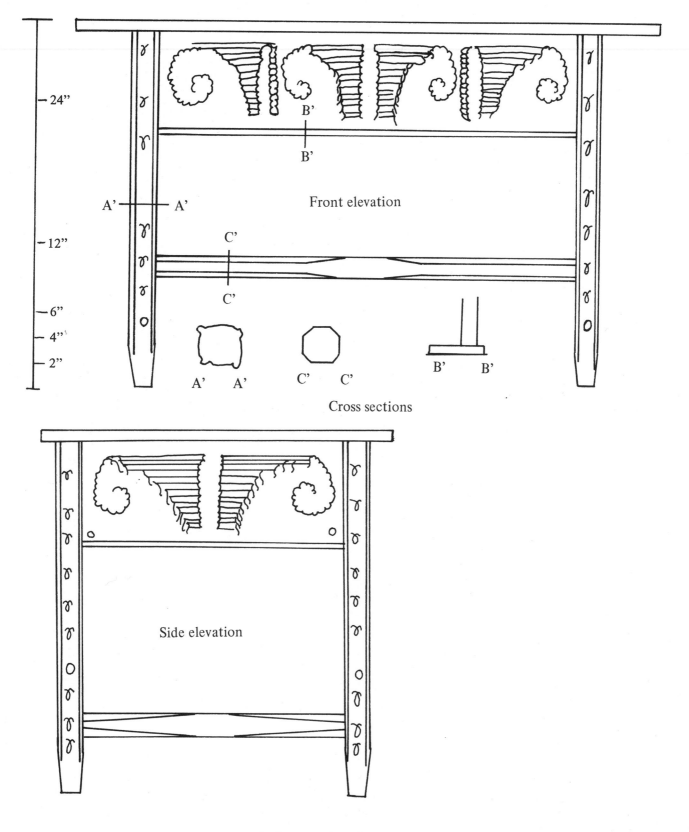

- 24"
- 12"
- 6"
- 4"
- 2"

B'
B'

A' — A'

Front elevation

C'
C'

A'   A'   C'   C'   B'   B'

Cross sections

Side elevation

TABLE - PENASCO AREA (C)

Drawn by Lumpkins

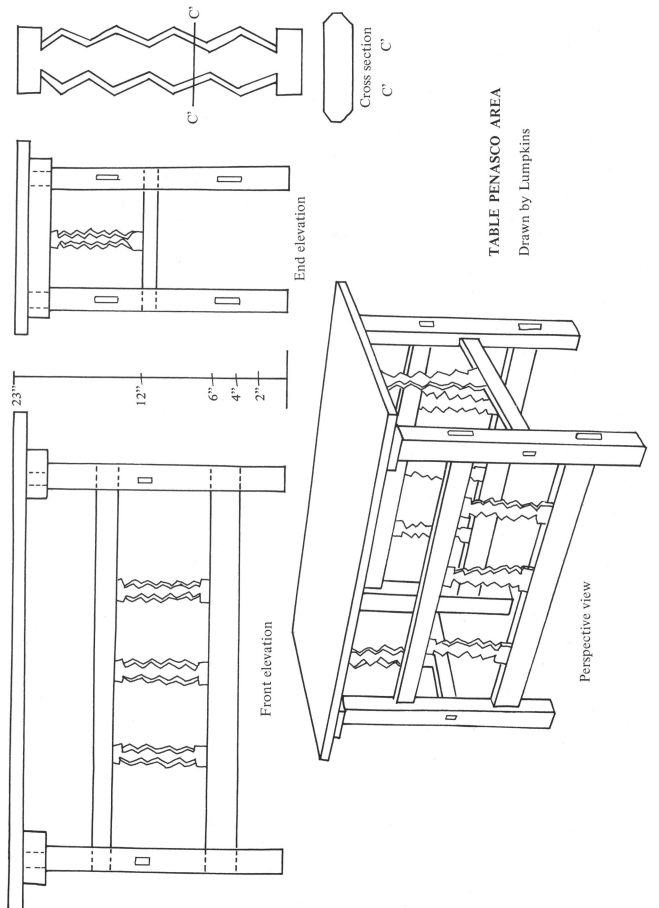

Cross section
C'   C'

End elevation

23"

12"

6"
4"
2"

Front elevation

TABLE PENASCO AREA
Drawn by Lumpkins

Perspective view

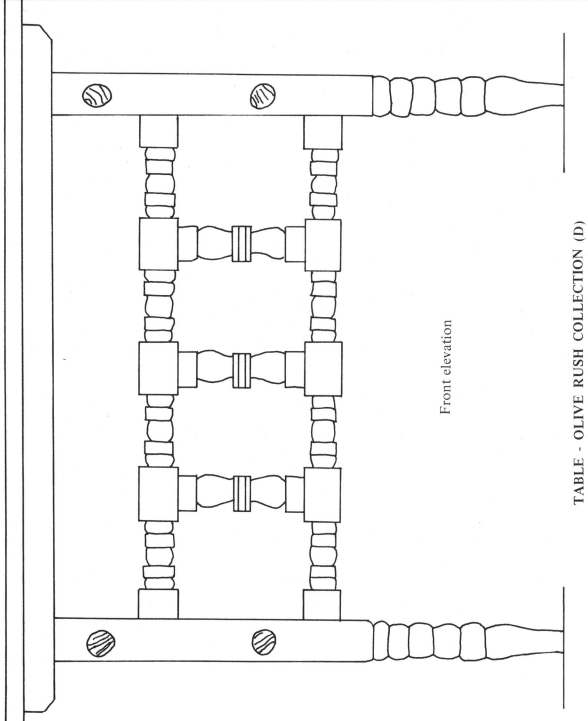

Front elevation

TABLE - OLIVE RUSH COLLECTION (D)

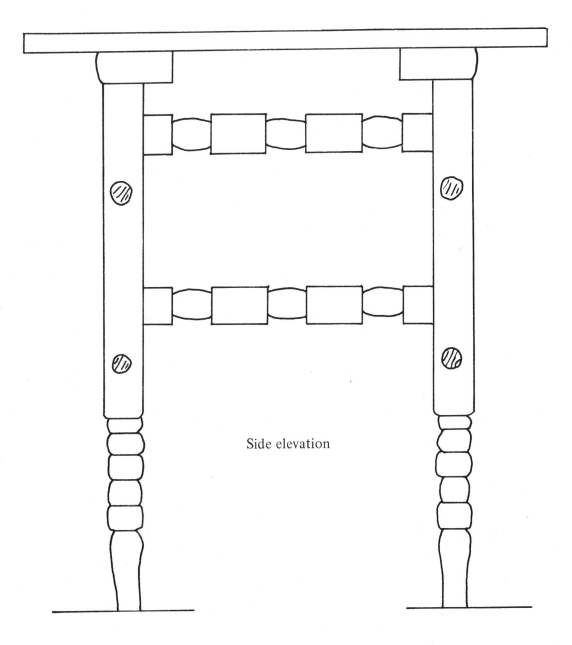

Side elevation

TABLE - OLIVE RUSH COLLECTION (D)

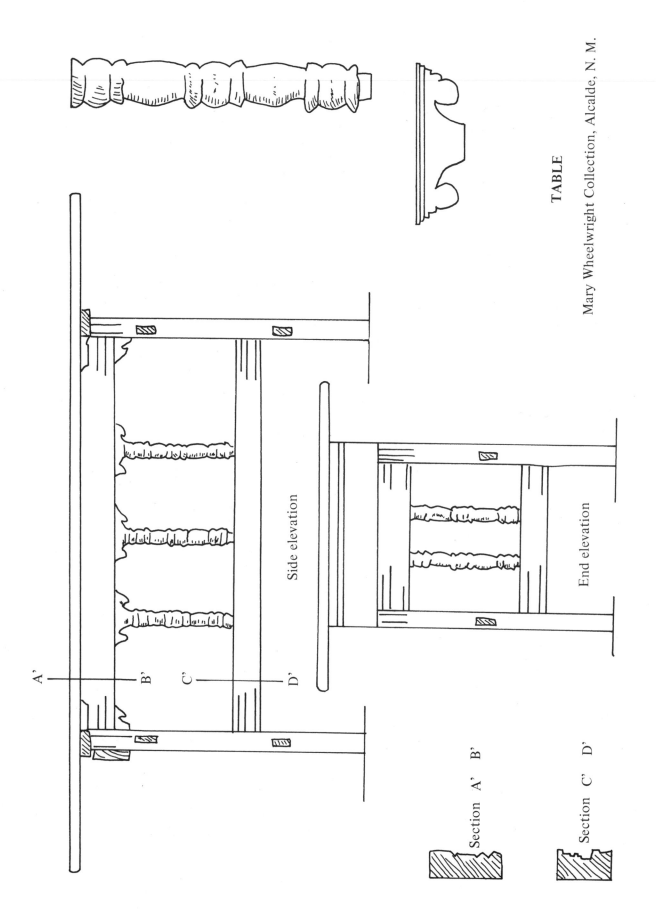

Side elevation

End elevation

A'

B'

C'

D'

Section A' B'

Section C' D'

TABLE

Mary Wheelwright Collection, Alcalde, N. M.

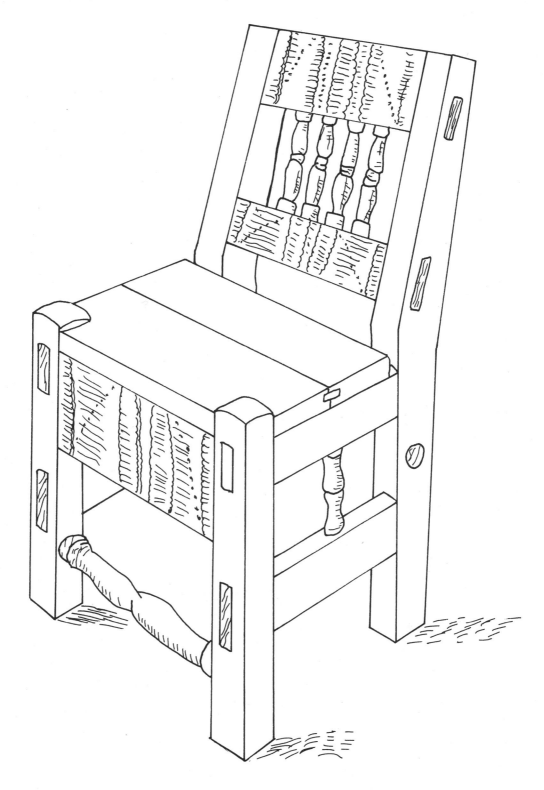

CHAIR (A)

Perspective view

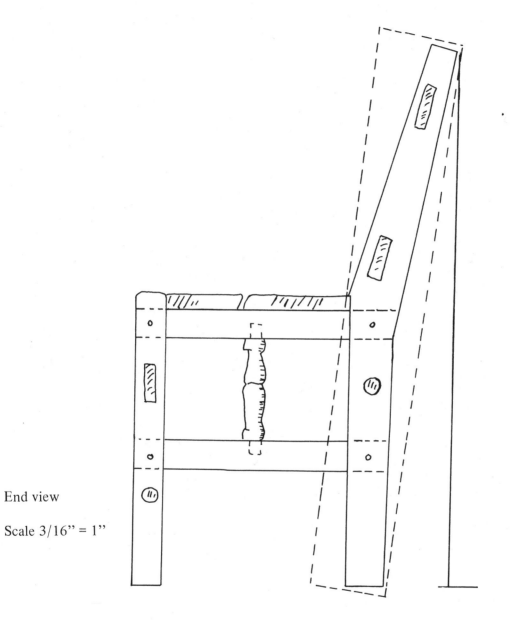

End view

Scale 3/16" = 1"

CHAIR (A)

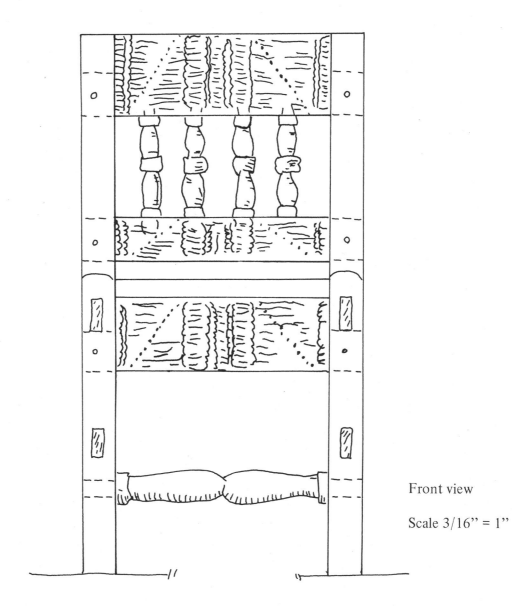

Front view

Scale 3/16" = 1"

CHAIR (A)

Notice slight narrowing

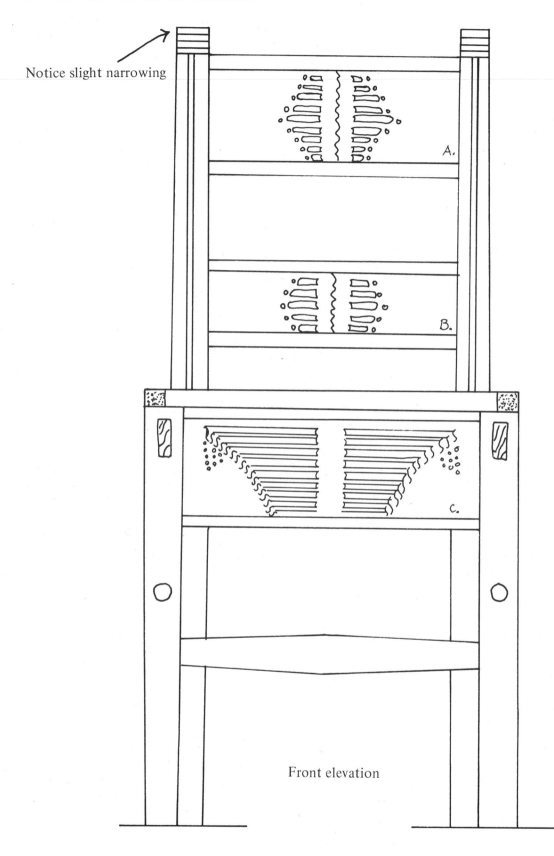

A.

B.

C.

Front elevation

CHAIR (B)

Culvert Collection, Taos, N. M.

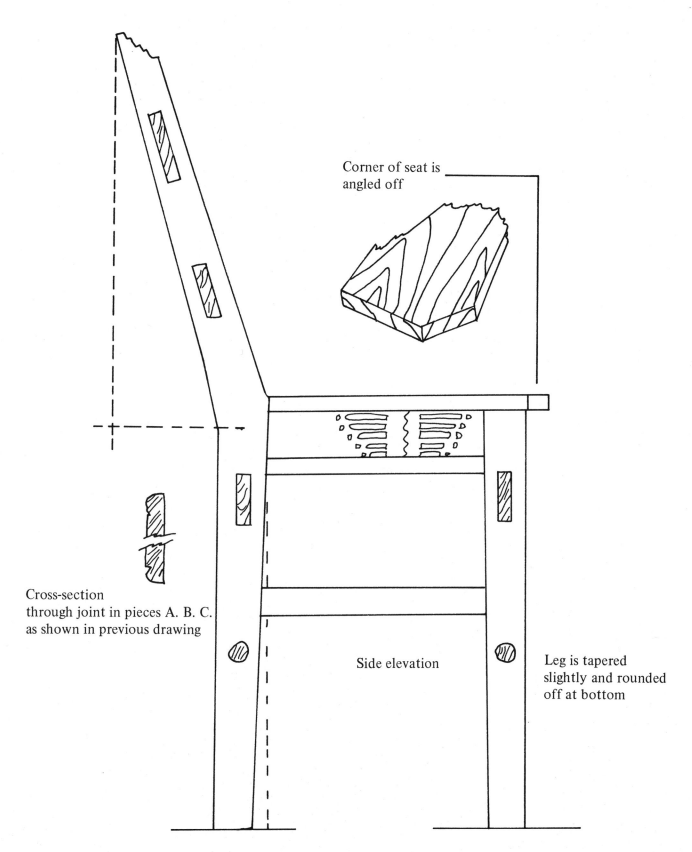

Corner of seat is
angled off

Cross-section
through joint in pieces A. B. C.
as shown in previous drawing

Side elevation

Leg is tapered
slightly and rounded
off at bottom

CHAIR (B)
Culvert Collection, Taos, N. M.

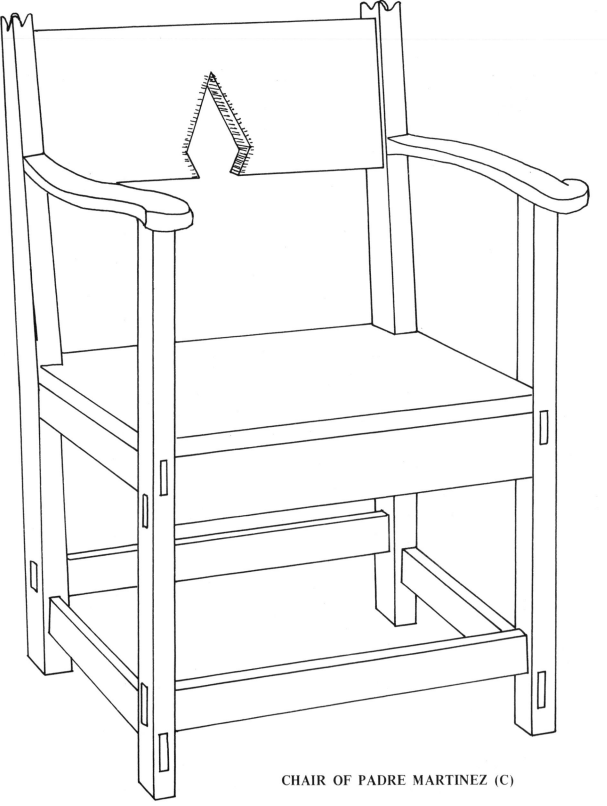

CHAIR OF PADRE MARTINEZ (C)

Perspective
Originally upholstered with cloth

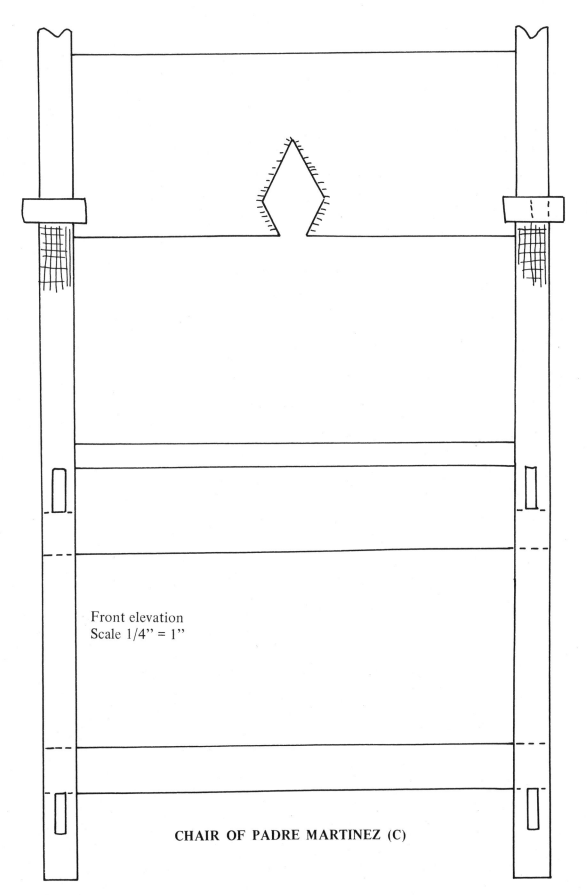

Front elevation
Scale 1/4" = 1"

CHAIR OF PADRE MARTINEZ (C)

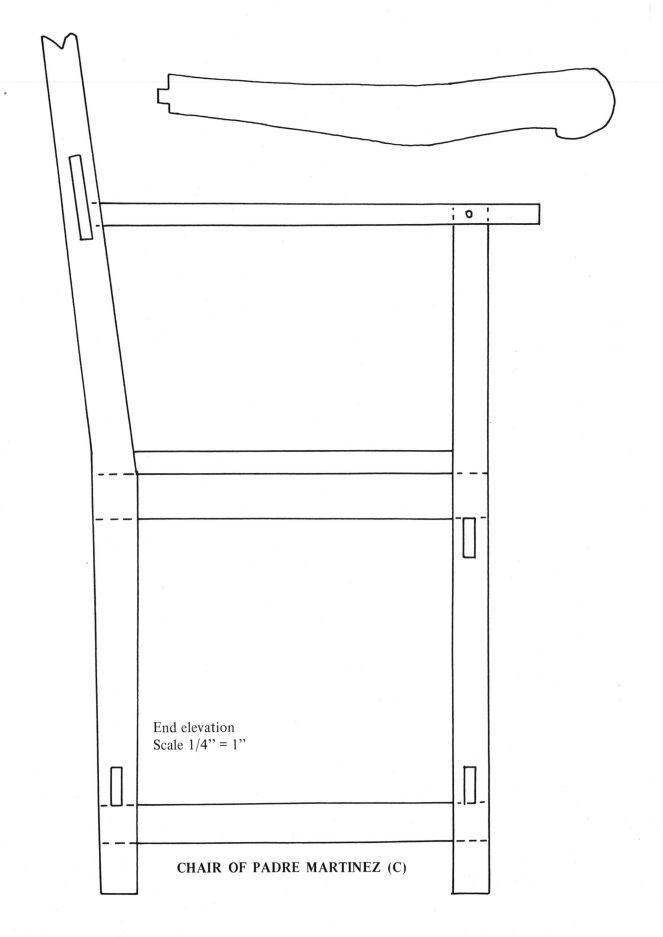

End elevation
Scale 1/4" = 1"

CHAIR OF PADRE MARTINEZ (C)

OLD SPANISH CHAIR (D)

Perspective view
Scale 1/4" = 1"

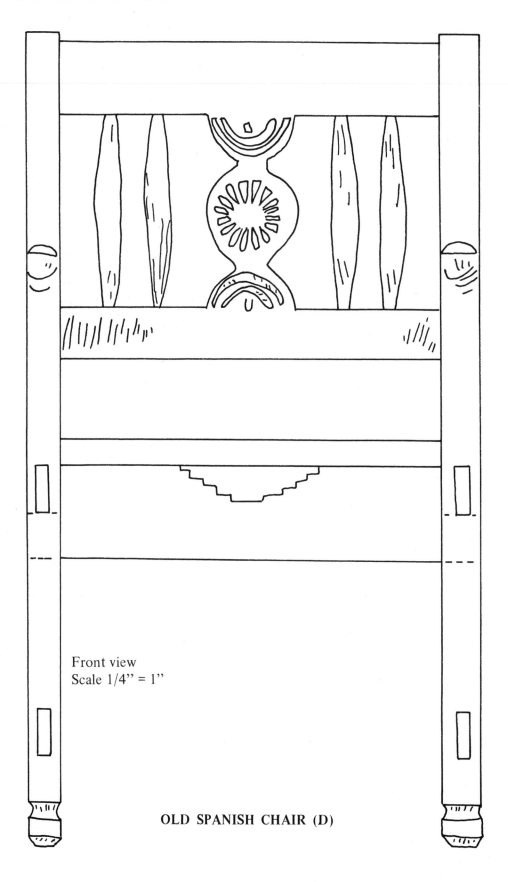

Front view
Scale 1/4" = 1"

OLD SPANISH CHAIR (D)

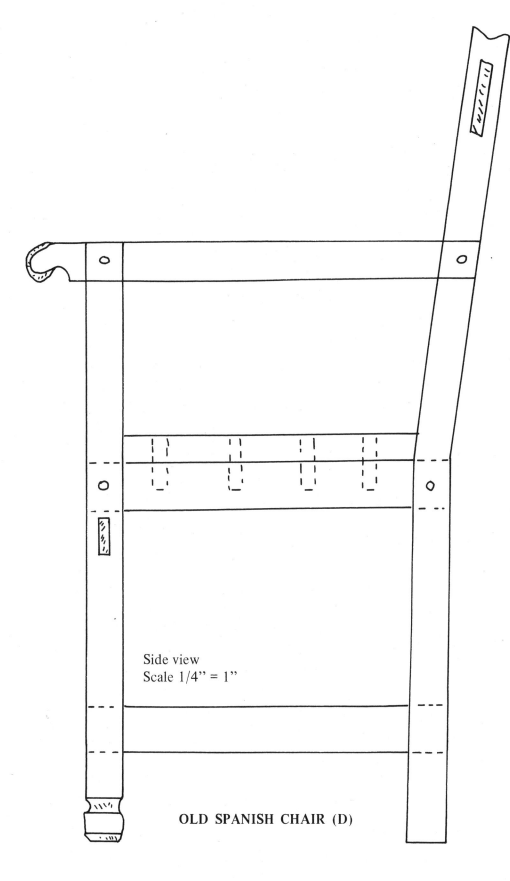

Side view
Scale 1/4" = 1"

OLD SPANISH CHAIR (D)

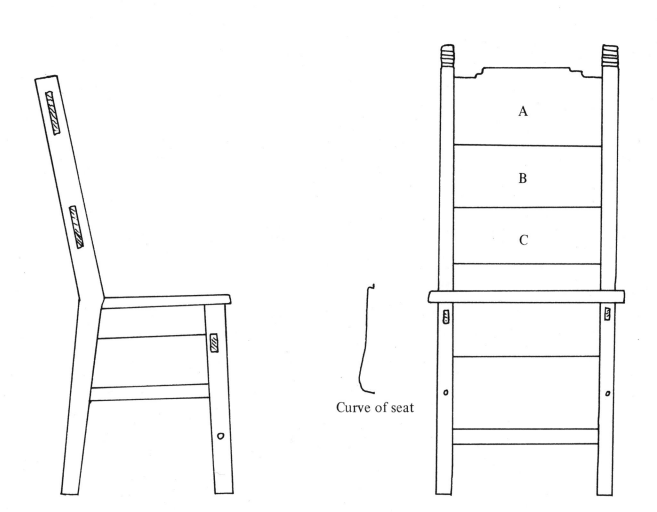

Curve of seat

Scale 1/8" = 1"

See next page for decorative details

CHAIR - APPLEGATE COLLECTION (E)

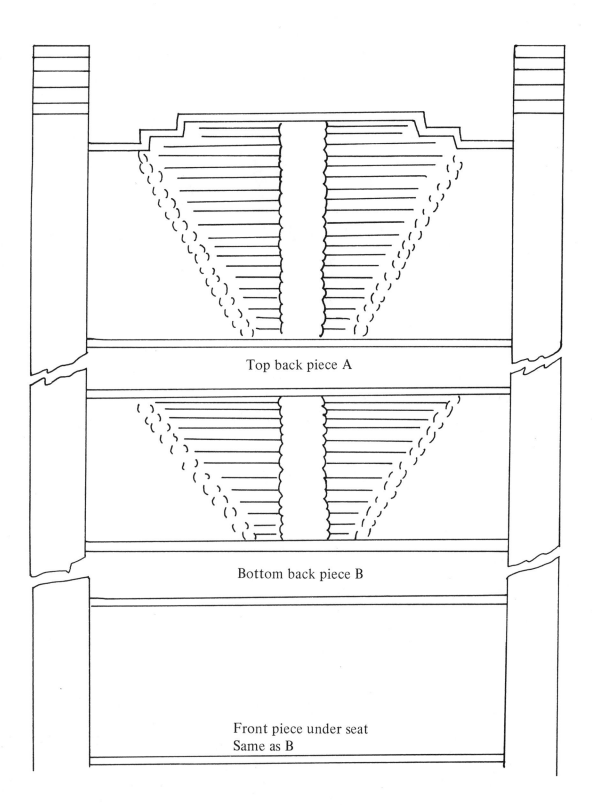

Top back piece A

Bottom back piece B

Front piece under seat
Same as B

CHAIR - APPLEGATE COLLECTION (E)

Decorative details
Scale 3/8" = 1"

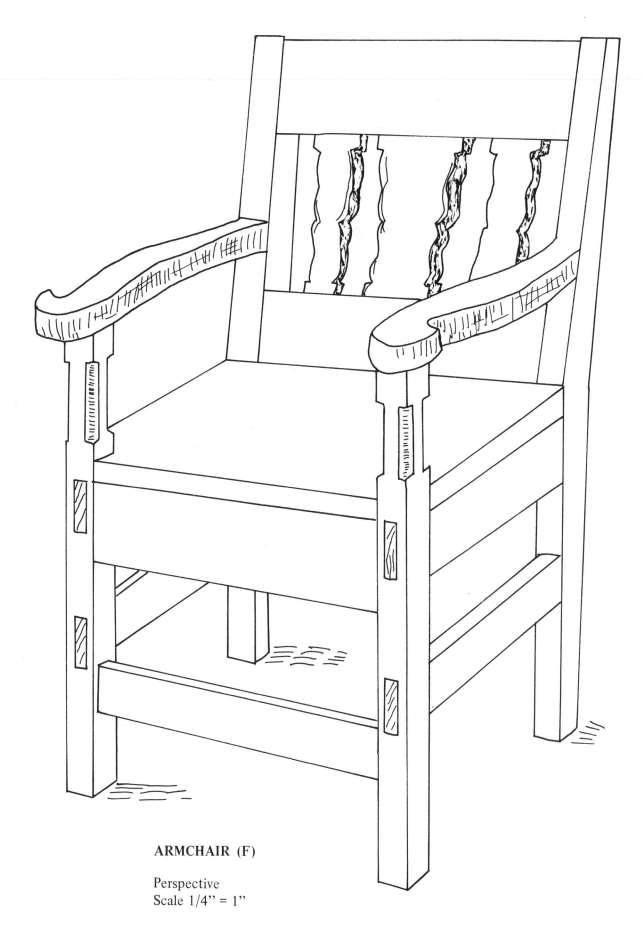

ARMCHAIR (F)

Perspective
Scale 1/4" = 1"

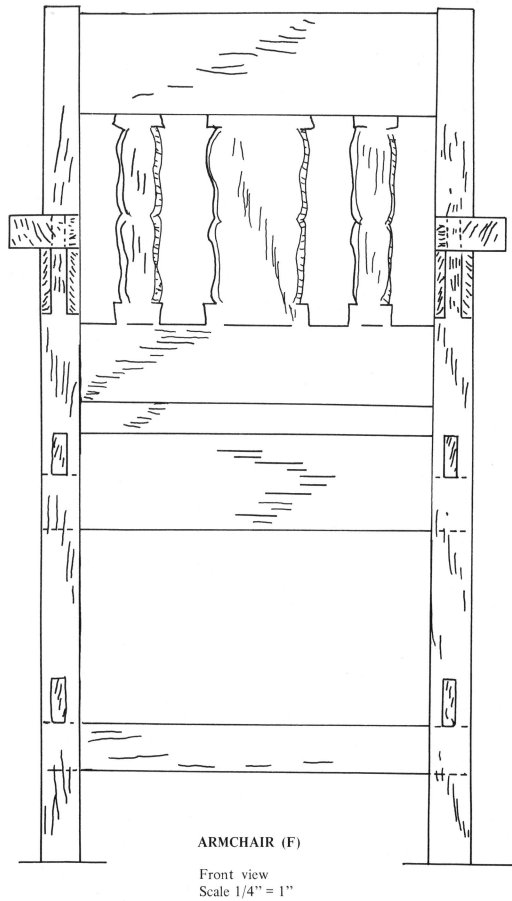

ARMCHAIR (F)

Front view
Scale 1/4" = 1"

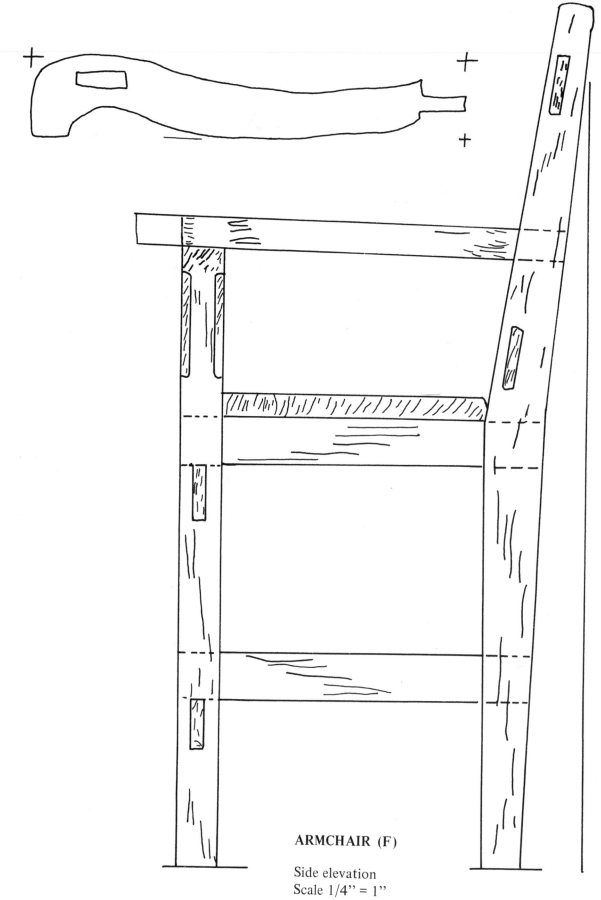

ARMCHAIR (F)

Side elevation
Scale 1/4" = 1"

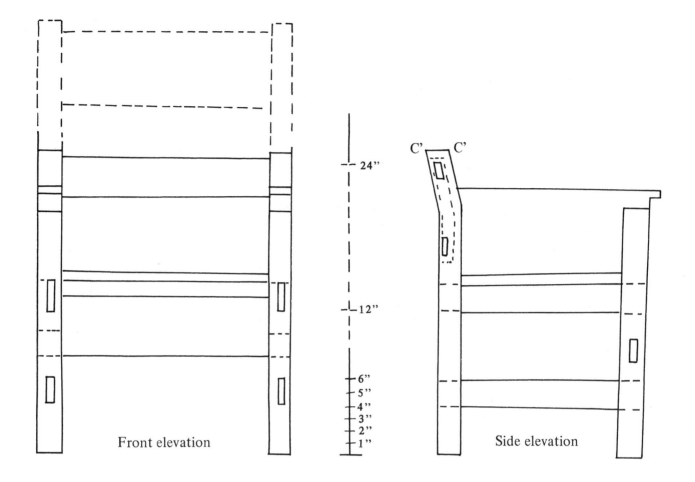

24"

12"

6"
5"
4"
3"
2"
1"

Front elevation

C'   C'

Side elevation

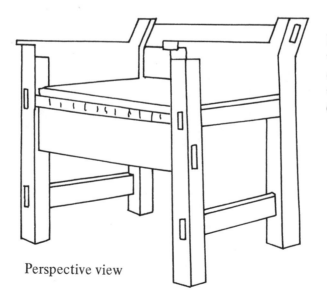

Perspective view

Note: The back
was higher at
one time but
was cut off at
C'–C' when recorded

CHAIR - PENASCO AREA
Drawn by Lumpkins

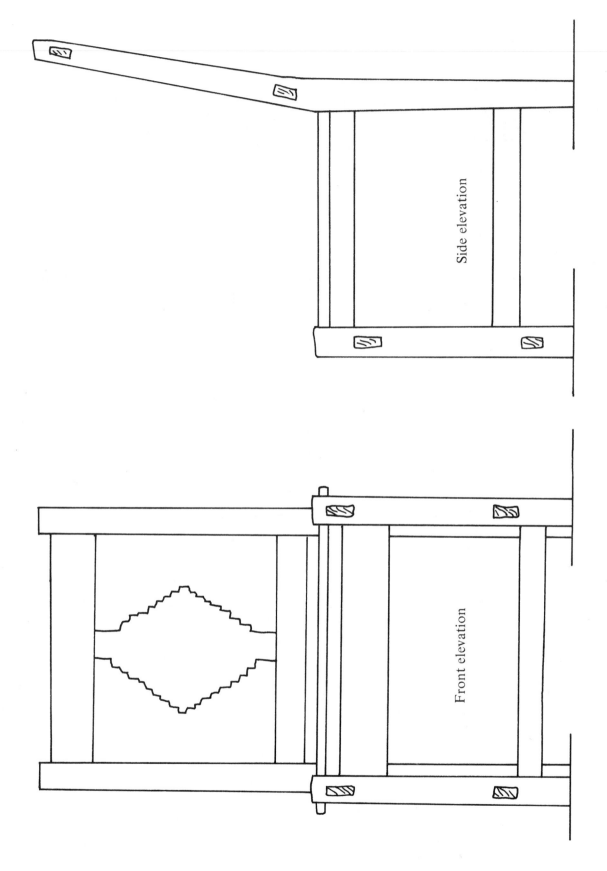

Side elevation

Front elevation

CHAIR

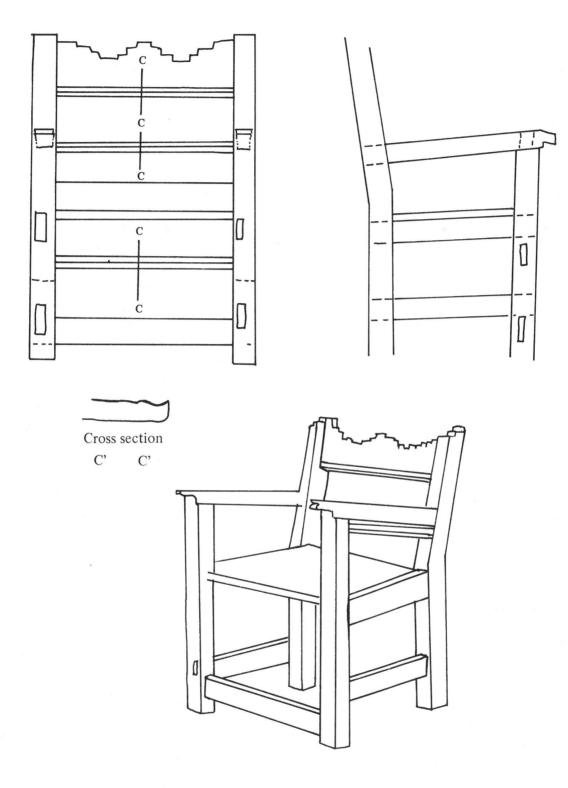

Cross section

C'   C'

CHAIR - PENASCO AREA

Drawn by Lumpkins

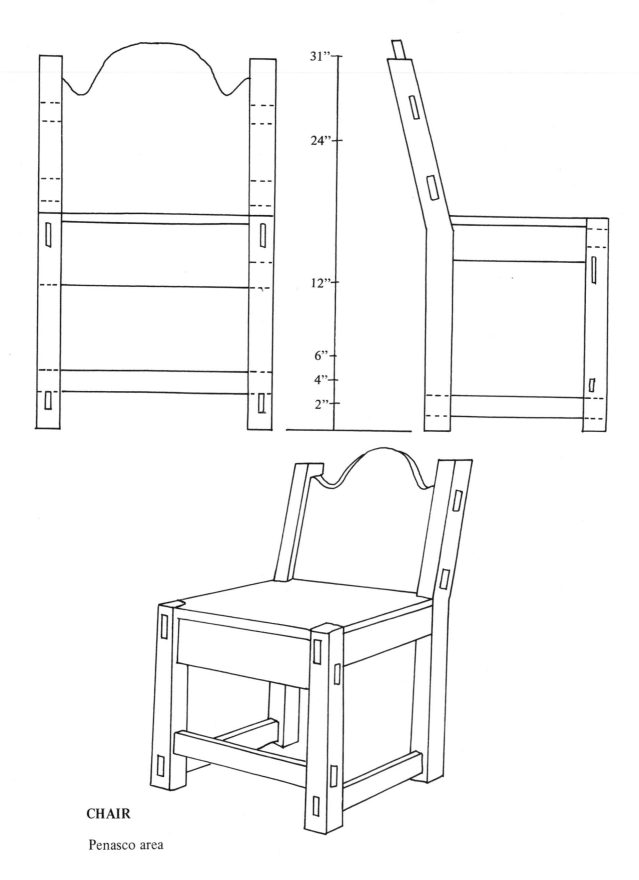

CHAIR

Penasco area

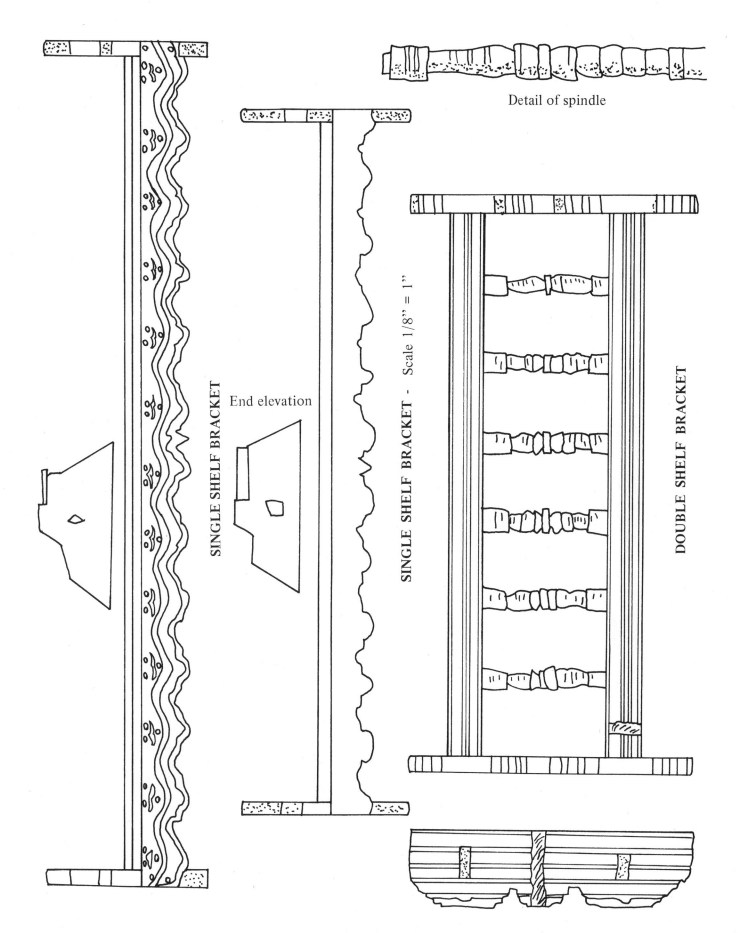

Detail of spindle

SINGLE SHELF BRACKET

End elevation

SINGLE SHELF BRACKET - Scale 1/8" = 1"

DOUBLE SHELF BRACKET

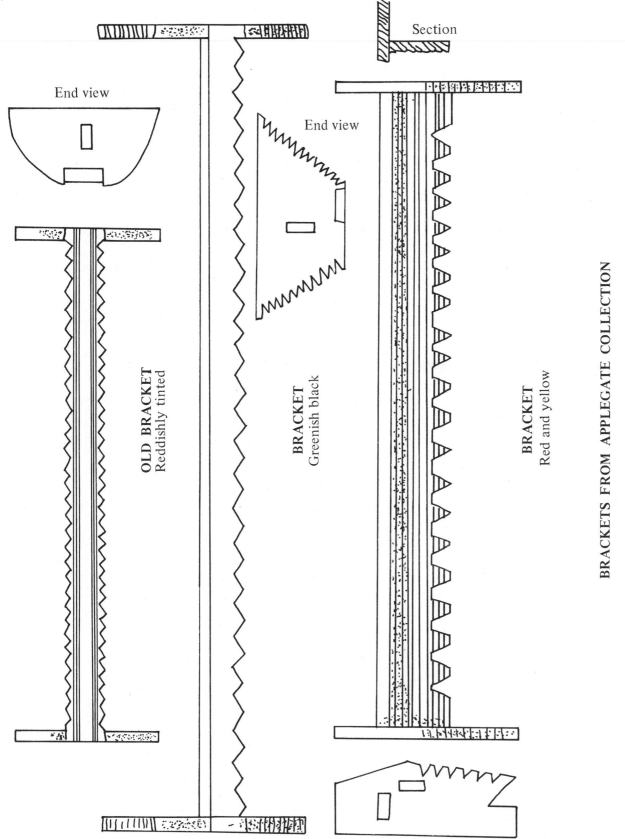

End view

Section

End view

OLD BRACKET
Reddishly tinted

BRACKET
Greenish black

BRACKET
Red and yellow

BRACKETS FROM APPLEGATE COLLECTION

Scale 1/8" = 1"

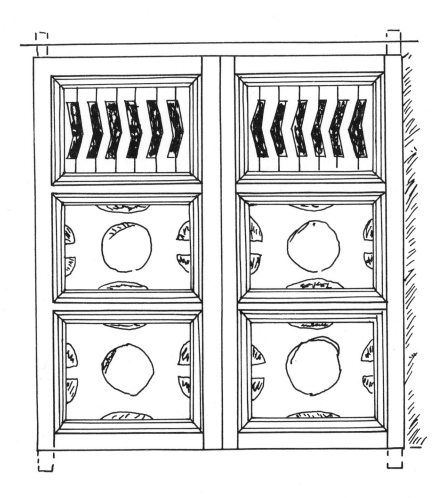

WALL CUPBOARD (A)

Front elevation
Scale 1/8" = 1"

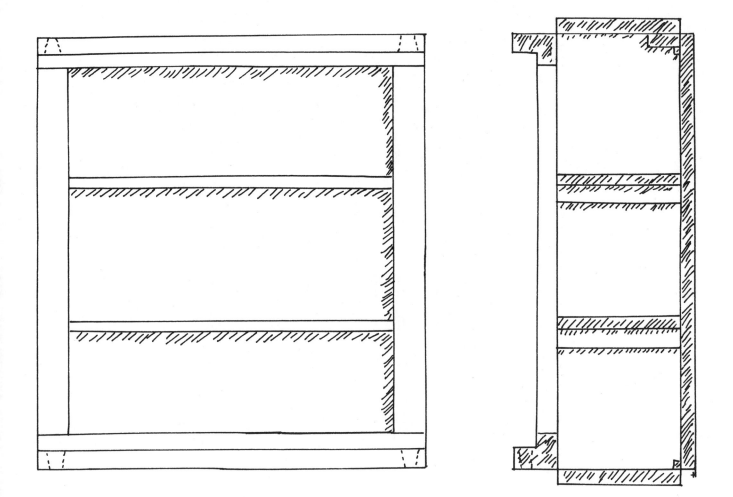

Scale 1/8" = 1"
Front elevation--
Doors removed

Sectional view

WALL CUPBOARD (A)

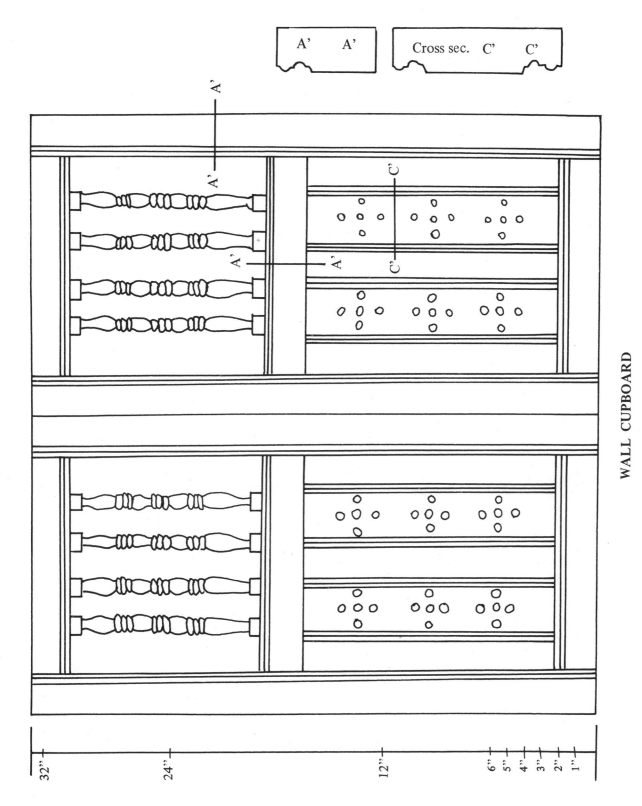

A'   A'

Cross sec.   C'   C'

WALL CUPBOARD

Penasco area

32"

24"

12"

6"
5"
4"
3"
2"
1"

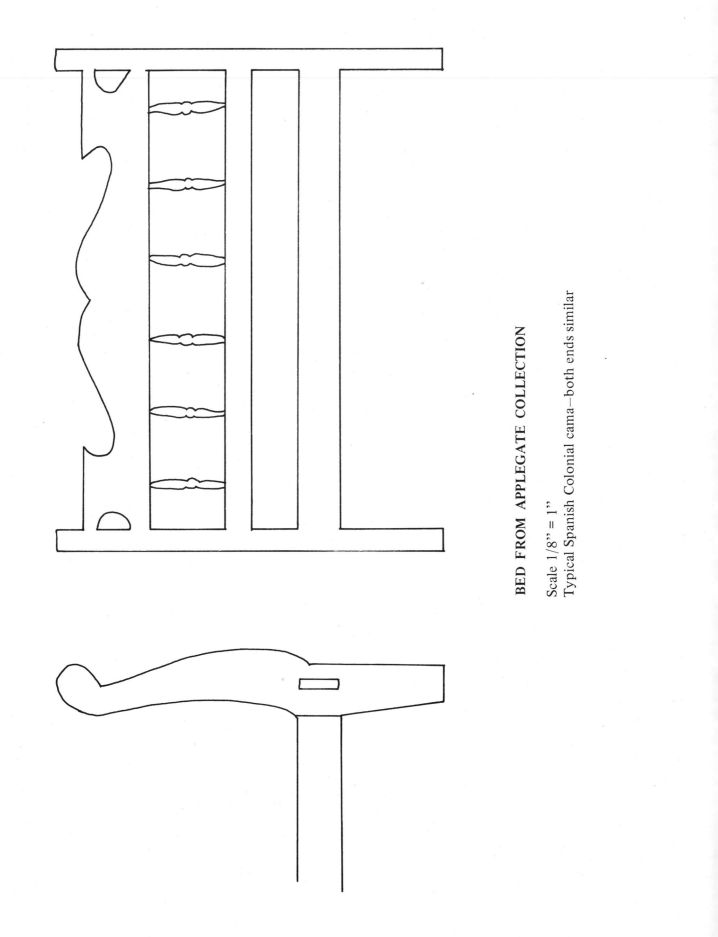

BED FROM APPLEGATE COLLECTION

Scale 1/8" = 1"
Typical Spanish Colonial cama—both ends similar

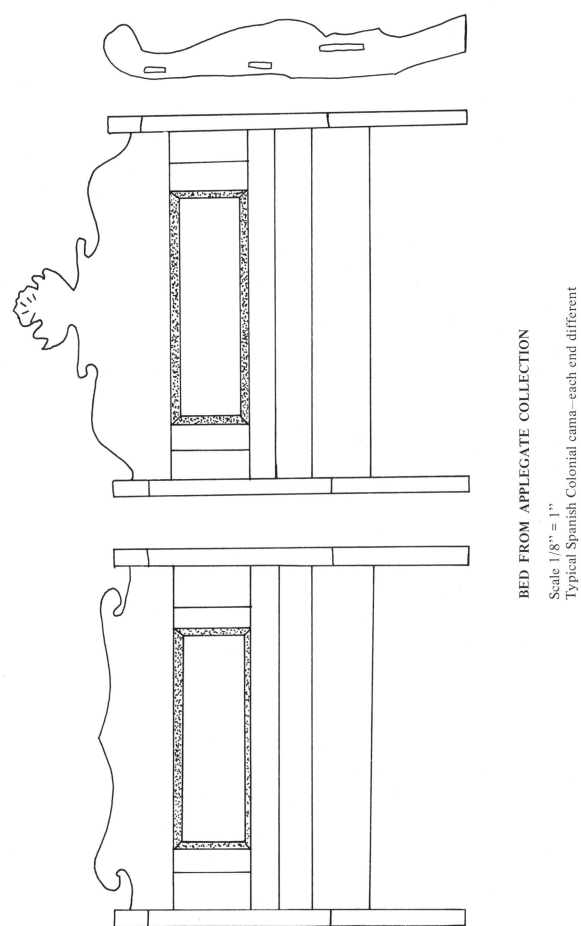

BED FROM APPLEGATE COLLECTION

Scale 1/8" = 1"
Typical Spanish Colonial cama—each end different

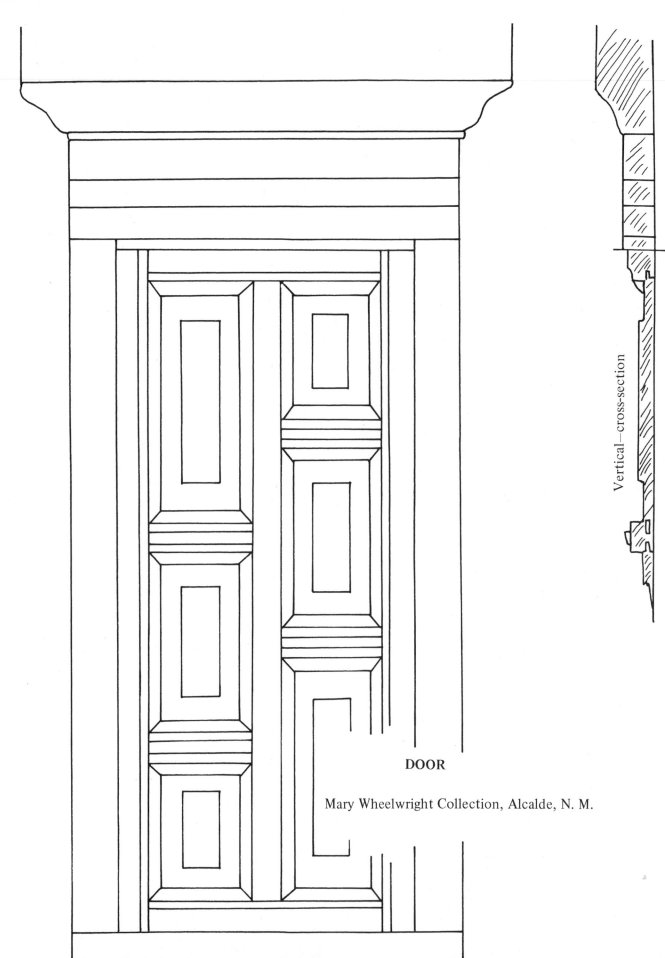

DOOR

Mary Wheelwright Collection, Alcalde, N. M.

Vertical—cross-section

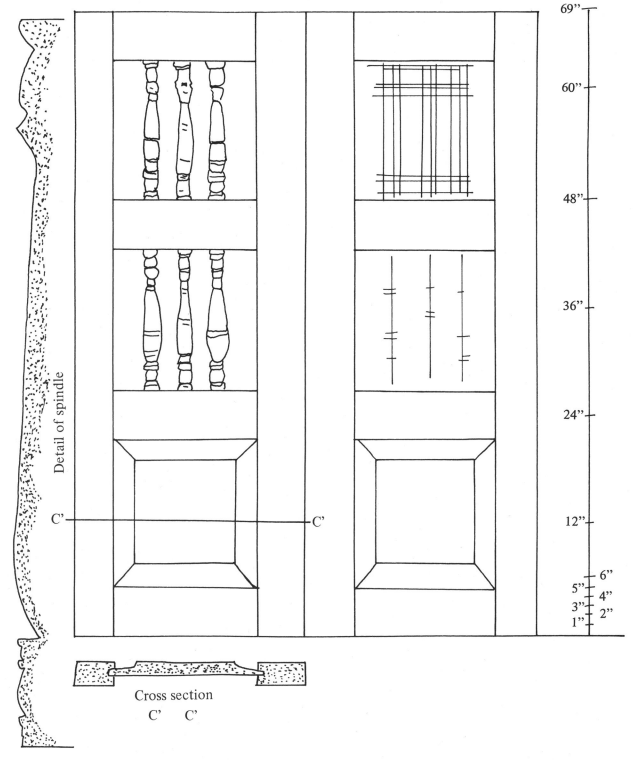

SPANISH COLONIAL DOORS

Penasco area
Drawn by Lumpkins

Vertical cross-section
through either panel

Vertical cross-section
through center

DOOR

Mary Wheelwright Collection, Alcalde, N. M.

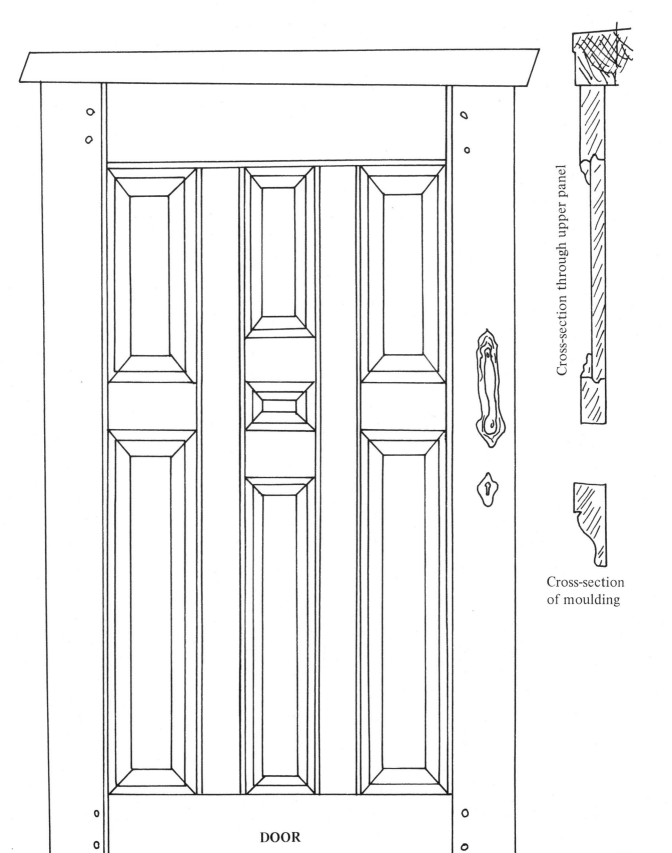

Cross-section through upper panel

Cross-section
of moulding

DOOR

Mary Wheelwright collection, Alcalde, New Mexico

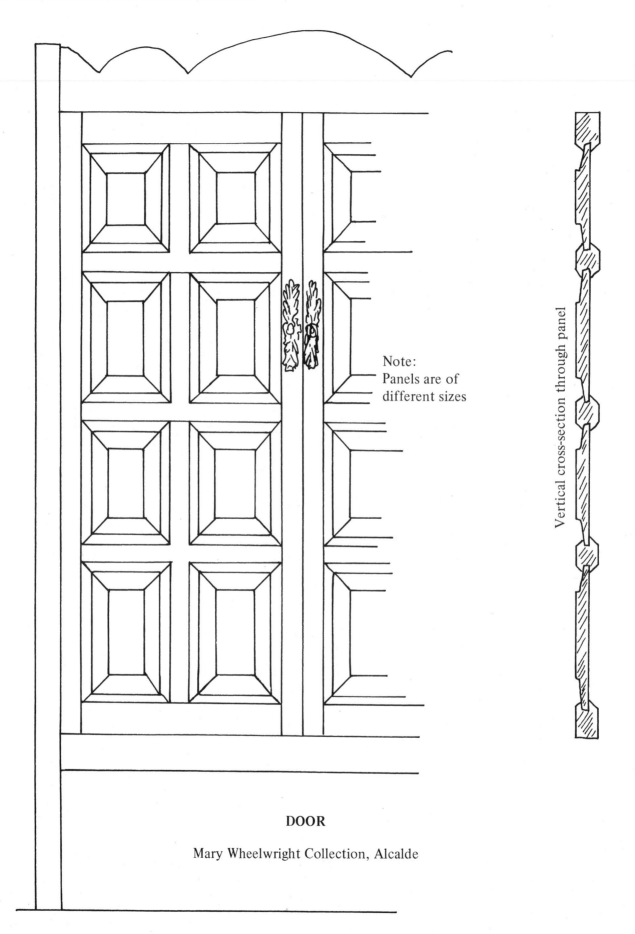

Note:
Panels are of
different sizes

Vertical cross-section through panel

DOOR

Mary Wheelwright Collection, Alcalde

End elevation

CARVED CHEST

Front elevation
Scale 1/8" = 1"

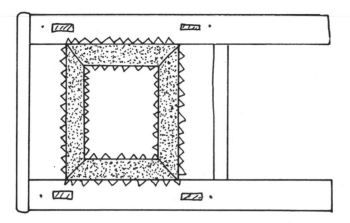

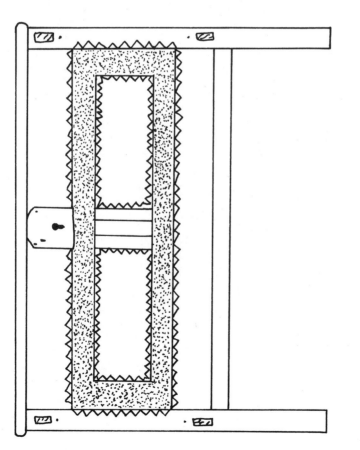

CHIP CARVED CHEST FROM APPLEGATE COLLECTION

Scale 1/8" = 1"

SPANISH COLONIAL CHEST

Penasco

36"

24"

12"

6"
5"
4"
3"
2"
1"

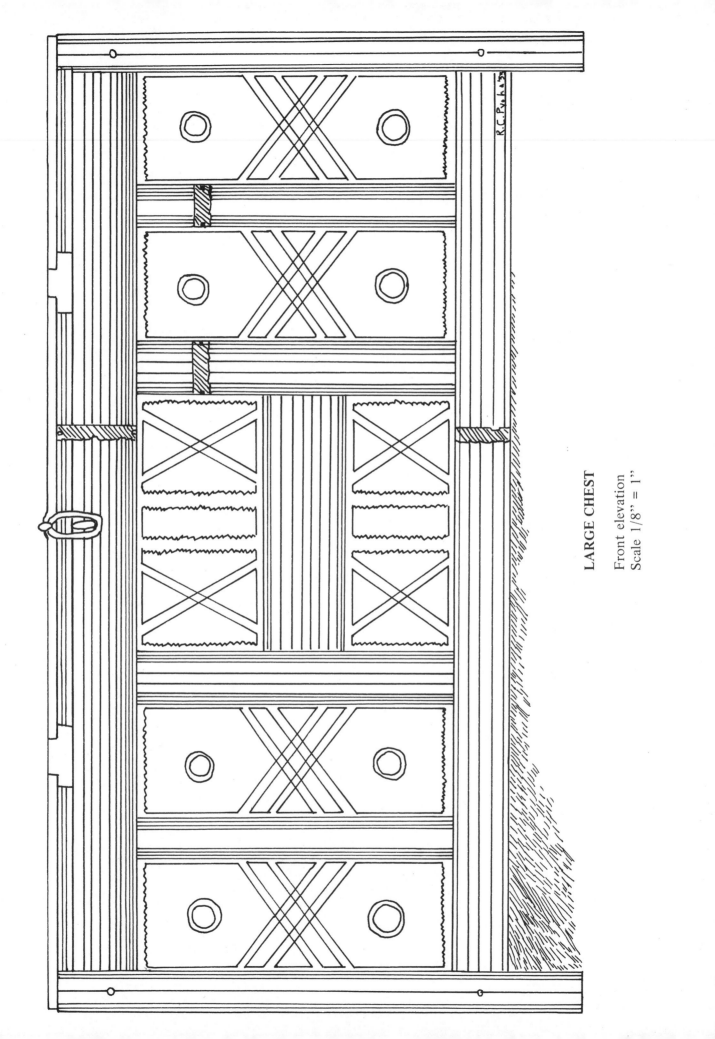

LARGE CHEST

Front elevation
Scale 1/8" = 1"

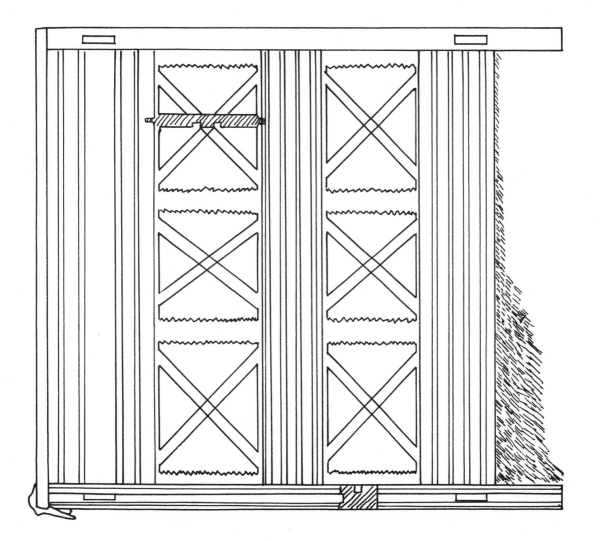

LARGE CHEST

End elevation
Scale 1/8" = 1"

CHEST ON STAND

Caja y tarima

Mary Wheelwright Collection, Alcalde, N. M.

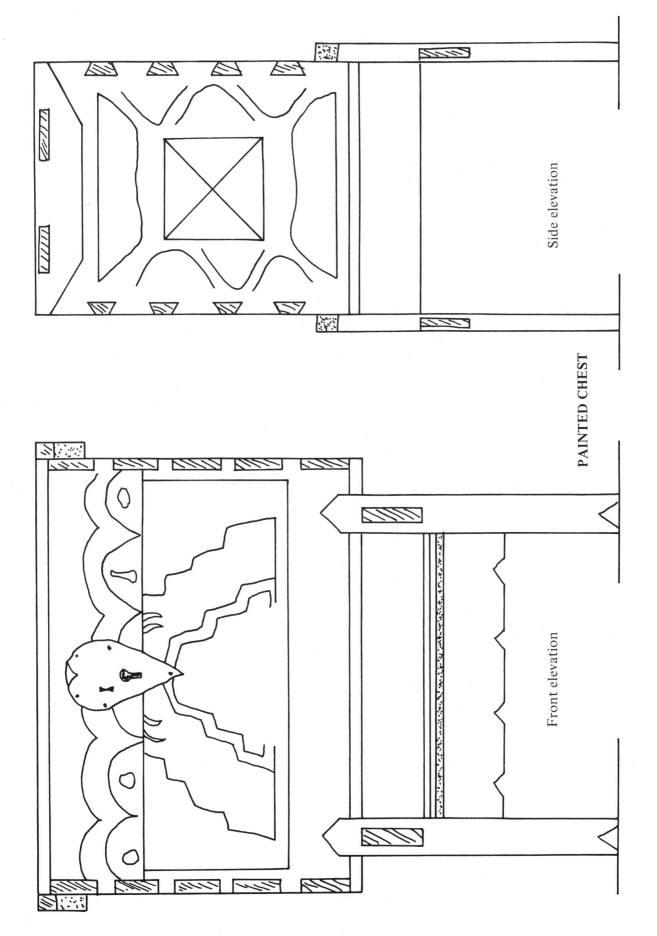

Side elevation

PAINTED CHEST

Front elevation

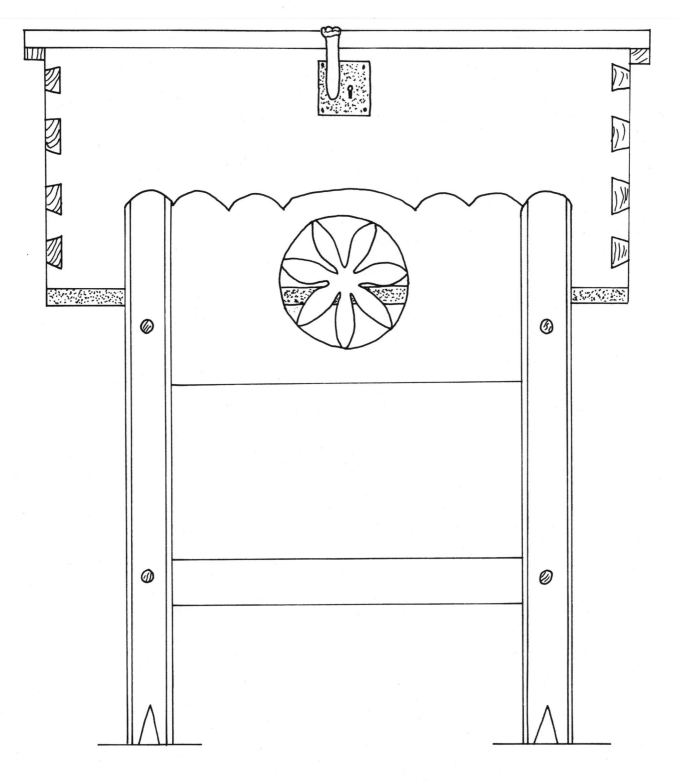

STAND FOR CHEST (A)

Olive Rush collection
Front elevation

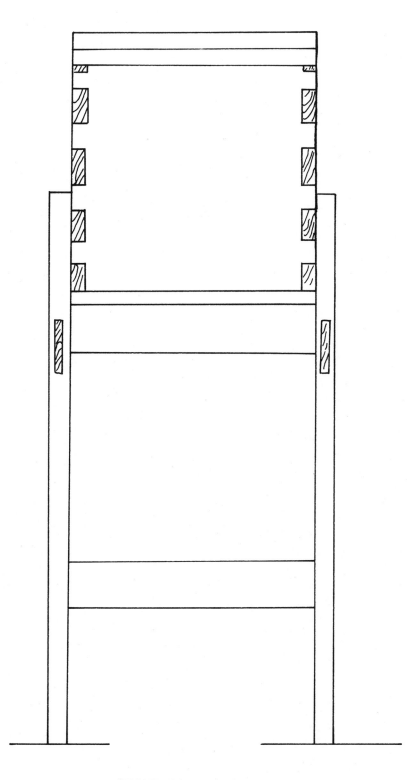

STAND FOR CHEST (A)

Olive Rush Collection
Side elevation

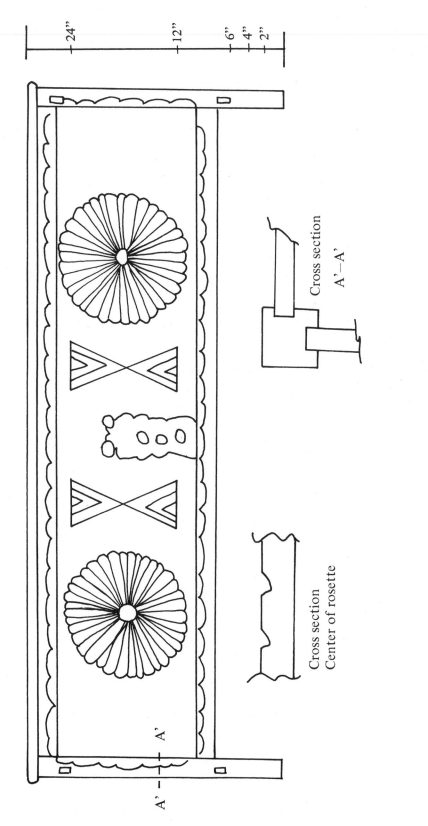

24"

12"

6"
4"
2"

Cross section
A'–A'

A'

Cross section
Center of rosette

A'

Design of rosette, "X", etc. stamped on wood with blunt tool 1/8" wide by 3/8" long. The design was then filled with black.

SPANISH COLONIAL CHEST AT PENASCO

VESTMENT CHEST

From old Pojoaque church carved about 1598
Lock of Spanish bronze

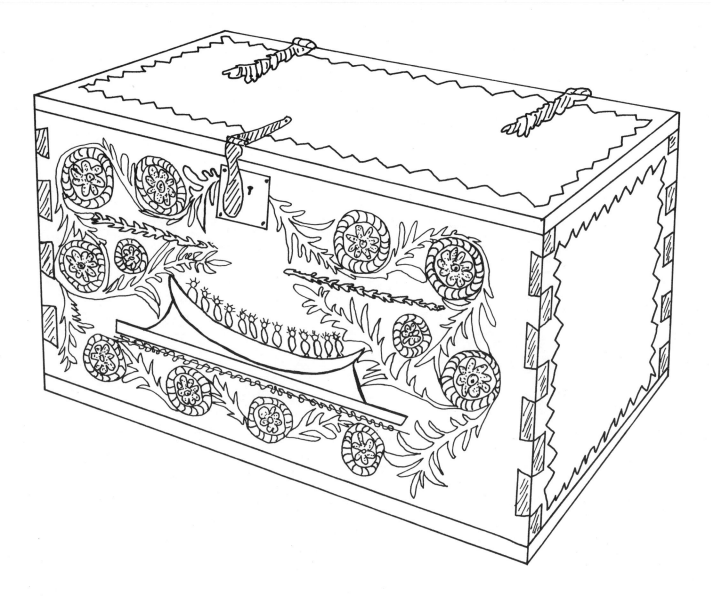

PAINTED CHEST

Mary Wheelwright Collection, Alcalde, N. M.

PAINTED CHEST FROM APPLEGATE COLLECTION

Scale 1/8" = 1"

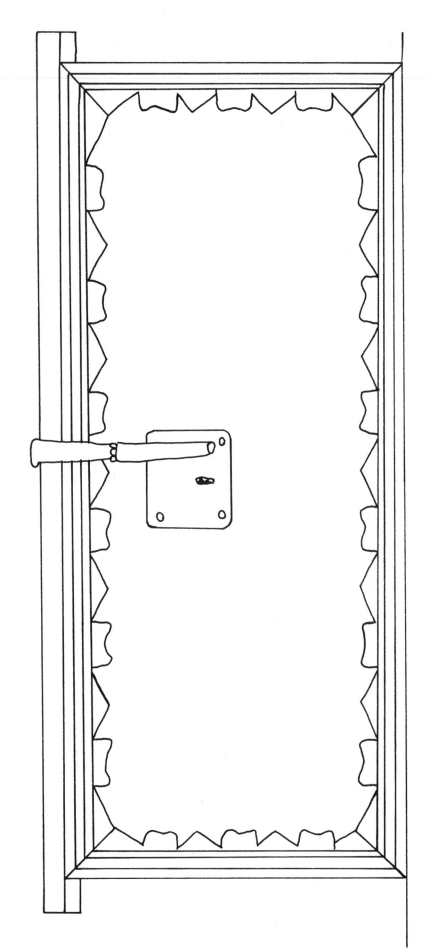

CHEST

Bouquet Ranch, Pojoaque, N. M.

CHEST

Bouquet Ranch, Pojoaque, N. M.

Cross section through moulding

Cross section through moulding

Side elevation

Front elevation

CHEST

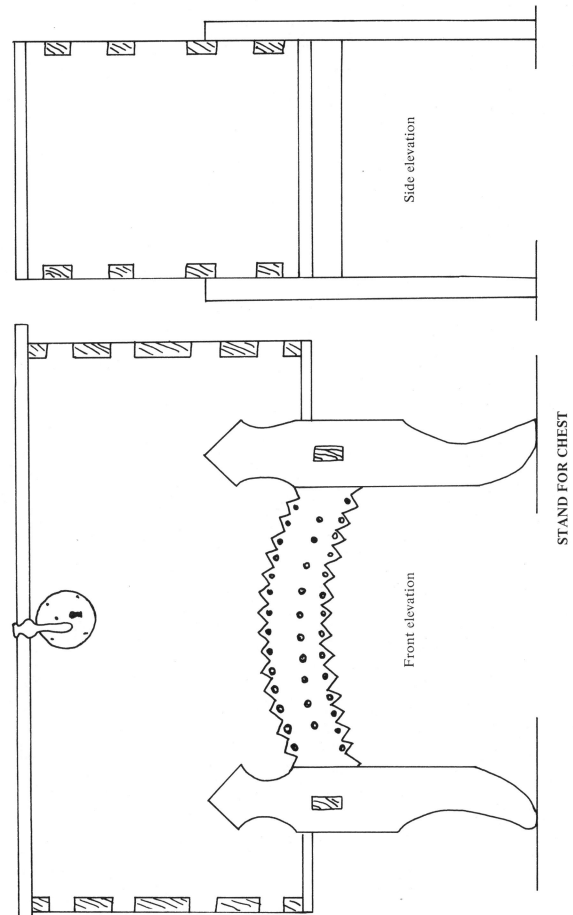

Side elevation

STAND FOR CHEST

Mary Wheelwright Collection, Alcalde, N. M.

Front elevation

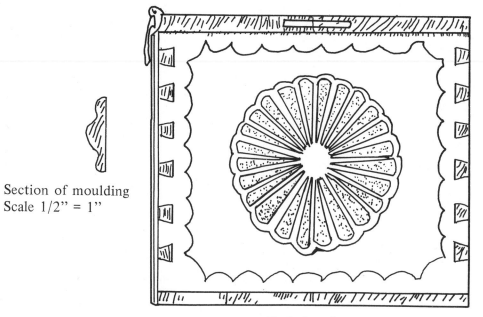

Section of moulding
Scale 1/2" = 1"

End elevation

Front elevation
Scale 1/8" = 1"

CHEST (B)

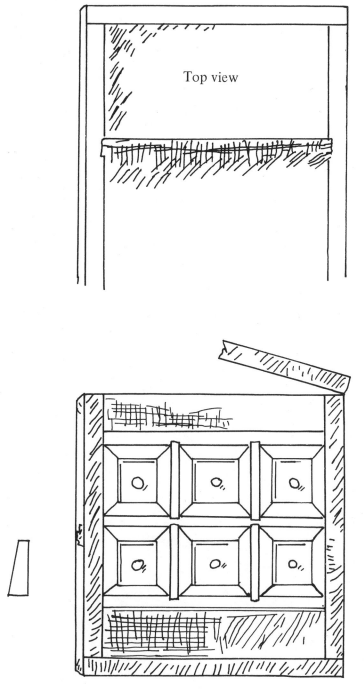

Top view

Moulding
Actual size

Cross-section showing drawers

Showing interior—end and top views
Scale 1/8" = 1"

CHEST (B)

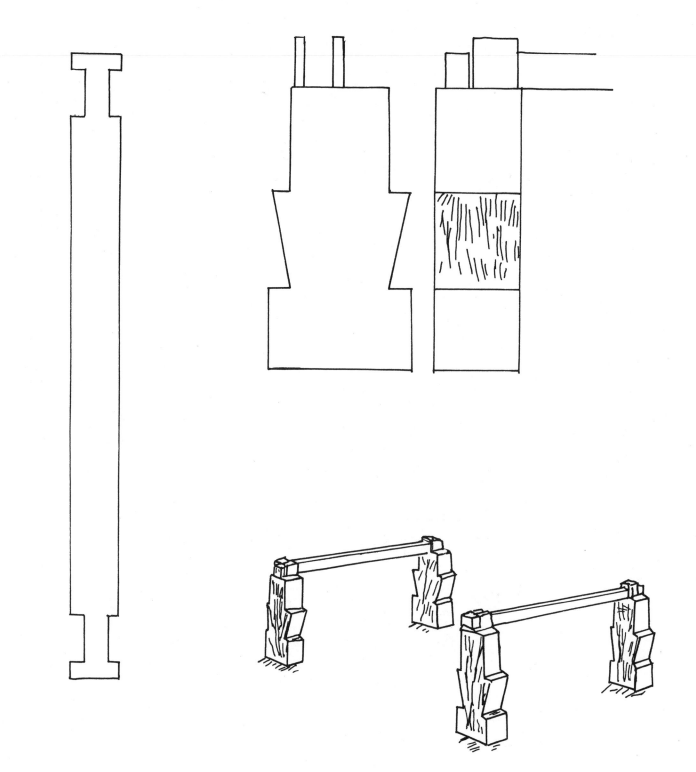

TRUNK RACK

Scale 1/4" = 1"

SPANISH COLONIAL PAINTED CHESTS

The drawings in this pamphlet were made from examples in museums and private collections [of Carlos Vierra, Olive Rush, Sheldon Parsons, Brice H. Sewell, The Hamilton Collection, and The Spanish & Indian Trading Company]. The motifs have been reproduced as accurately as possible, although it is difficult to simulate the richness and beauty of the colors which are to be found in this type of decoration that age has mellowed to a harmonious ensemble. The palette of these early artists was limited to the natural colors of the iron oxides—yellow, red and brown tones and the vegetable blue of indigo. Cochineal may have been used for a bright red. The base, or undercoat, was yeso or jaspe, a native white gypsum, and was mixed with glue produced from cow horns. This undercoat was painted on the raw wood in several coats. In some cases, the artisan has apparently smoothed the successive layers by rubbing with soft pumice rock which is abundant in New Mexico. The medium of the colors was mixed with either glue water or the yolk of an egg. This substance served to keep the paint in place so effectively that examples known to be over two hundred years old show practically no disintegration.

In Old Mexico and Spain, the painted chests were necessary articles of furniture in all households, except in those of the very poor. In Mexico we find brilliant chests of lacquer imported from China in the days of the China trade, and later many beautiful examples were produced in Guerrero and Michoacan, noted for their fine lacquer and painted work. These chests were lavish in color and decoration, while New Mexican chests take a more simple form both in color and design. On New Mexico chests, most of the decoration is placed on the front and sides and very little on the top.

The designs show Spanish influence and in some instances record historical happenings in Spanish history both in the old world and in Old Mexico. The "El Toreo," or bull fight, is a motif frequently used. Another motif which is quite common is one showing a group of noblemen or soldiers in uniform, with plumed helmets, in a boat with many oars. The use of the rosette is somewhat common, as well as conventionalized floral designs combined with human and animal figures. The foliage in many cases is not related to the floral motifs which are used, the artist being more interested in decoration than realism. On a number of chests, the chalice or sacramental cup is used as a center of the pattern.

The wood used in the chests is thin and the chests vary in size, having the approximate dimensions of 28 inches in length, 16 inches in width and 18 inches in depth. The lid is generally fastened with iron staples and hasps and the **chapa**, or lock, was simple and nicely wrought.

Judging from the brush strokes, the decoration resembled oil paint and may have been made from resin mixed with a small quantity of animal fats. In many instances, the wood was coated with yeso or jaspe, the same as the foundation used in the older altar decorations. The decoration is more sophisticated than that found in the **reredos**, or altar screen, and that leads to the conclusion that they were produced at a somewhat later period.

During colonial times, it was customary for the bride to own a painted chest to hold her dowry and personal finery. There may have been many such chests but few now remain for study.

As to the origin of these chests, there is very little definite knowledge available. In the native families where they are owned, it is known only that they have been in their possession for many years, handed down from one generation to another. Those owned by the Anglos were purchased from itinerant traders who, in most cases, obtained them by bartering cheap machine-made articles. According to tradition, it may be safely judged that most of the chests were made over one hundred years ago.

Some authorities have thought that they were possibly brought from Old Mexico as containers for imported goods such as coffee, chocolate and silks. This supposition is based on the fact that they are of a size which would be convenient as boxes to be loaded on either side of a mule.

However, Carlos Vierra, veteran artist and collector of New Mexican crafts, is of the opinion that they were made in New Mexico. He bases his conclusion on the following facts:

First, that these chests show very little mark of wear and tear such as would be caused by pack ropes, and there is no scuffing of the bottoms which would be caused if brought by wagon train.

Second, that the wood is of native pine, while in Mexico they would probably have been made of a more valuable and substantial wood.

Third, that the similarity of design and technique used in the paintings would point to the probability that they were made by either one artist or his family; however, he may have employed apprentices. Mr. Vierra also states that the skilled and finished technique as well as the deft handling of design and pigments, leads him to believe that the artist was trained in Spain or at least by a European master in Mexico, later coming to New Mexico to practice his trade.

As a rule, the color background on these chests is either black, dark green or a sienna red. In the design we find red, blue, sienna, umber and green with the various stages of shading and with a lavish use of white. Iron locks, hasps and hinges complete the decoration.

Chest Number 1, from the collection of Brice H. Sewell, has a background of reddish sienna and is symbolical in design and color. We find a definite religious influence here. A golden chalice or sacramental cup filled with sprouting, delicate wheat forms the center motif. The chalice in Christian art is a symbol of faith, the sprouting wheat a symbol of fertility. On either side of the chalice are two lovely blue birds, symbols of the soul. The flower rosette and leaves complete the design.

Chest Number 2, from the Carlos Vierra collection, shows a colonial lady with her powdered hair fixed high on her head, riding in a coach reminiscent of Maximilian days. Her lackey and coachman accompany her. The whole arrangement of design is more worldly and the treatment of the figures a naive and pleasing one. The color background of the chest is a golden red, mellow with time. The combinations of yellows, blues and reds shaded with white present a pleasing scene.

Chest background—golden red, inner border dark blue, lines white

Rosettes—background brick red, sides dark red, tips white, dots dark red

Leaves on right and left sides—dark green edged in white, white dots, puffs
     golden yellow, center brown, small puffs dark red, lines dark red

Leaves on top and bottom—dark green edged in white, puffs yellow with
     brown centers, half moons black-blue, small ones red

Horse—white with black edges

Flowers in center—red with white edges

Chest Number 3, also from the Vierra collection, depicts a youth serenading his lady. In his hands he holds a stringed instrument. He sits on a large rock, his long, dangling legs encased in white stockings. The lady stands, oblivious to all. She wears a white gown, approaching an empire style. Along with the flower design, the floral treatment combines a berry-like design. A geometrical border outlines the motif. The color background is a light sienna.

Chest background—sienna with white.

Leaves—dark blue edged in white, black lines through center, fine lines in black.

Flowers—brick red with fine lines in darker red edged with touches of white.

Man—blue coat, white shirt, blue trousers with white spots, white hose, black shoes.

Woman—dress white, lines and dots black.

Flowers in center—red with white.

Chest Number 4 is from the Parsons collection. The design on this chest takes on a farcical note. A buffoon mounted on a horse with long white horns gleefully displays his long mustachios. A dancing lady forms the center figure, while a bearded short-skirted figure dangles a rope-like article before her. The sienna golden background with the white and blue colors on the figures has a mellow and rich effect.

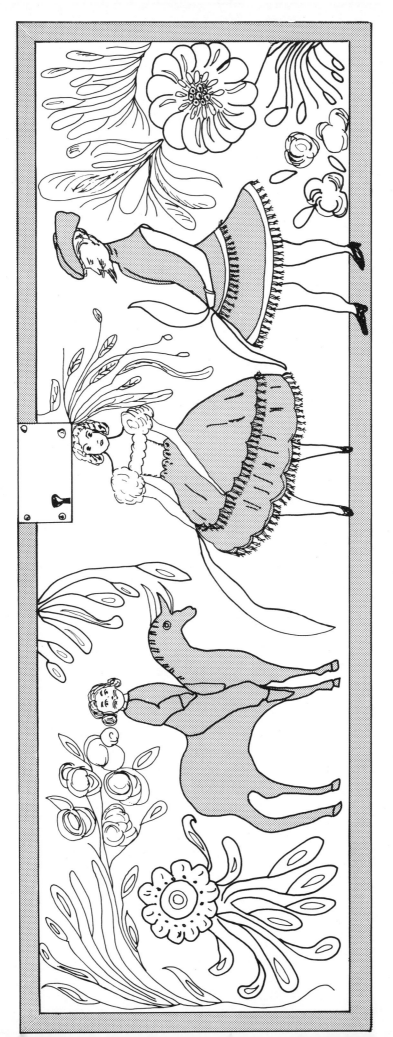

Chest Number 5, from the Olive Rush collection, shows a distinct "Toreo" influence. A horse with a bull's tail prances about, while a picador on his horse charges. A border of large rosettes and big leaves in black and sienna is simply and effectively used. This is one of the plainest of the chests. The only colors used are the variations of red, black and sienna.

Flowers—shaded sienna lines in black.

Outer leaves—black.

Inner leaves—shaded sienna.

Chest Number 6, from the Carlos Vierra collection, has a beautiful floral border with large rosettes of dark blue and red alternating in color and eight soldiers wearing their high "Shakos," military hats of that period, standing on a canoe. On either side are two colonial ladies elegantly dressed, with the royal decoration on the shoulder and across the front. The panniers on their gowns give a hooplike effect. Their high hair dress with flowers and feathers suggests the hair dress of the early eighteenth century.

Background of entire front of chest—black.

Leaf sprays outer border—dark green.

Rosettes—dark red alternating with dark blue ones; three rosettes marked "X" in golden brown.

Narrow inner border—dark blue with white dashes.

Spray (1)—leaves dark green, blue and red.

Gown (2)—blue; lines dark blue; gloves, panniers, shoulder decoration— light golden brown; hair—golden.

Rosette (3)—red shaded.

Spray (4)—dark red sienna and blue.

Boat (5)—sienna.

Soldiers (6)—trousers white; caps white; belt and blouse dark blue; shoulder straps brown; figures golden brown.

Puffs (7)—red, leaves blue and golden brown.

Gown (8)—yellowish red; lines dark red; panniers and shoulder decoration golden yellow; hair golden.

Spray (9)—same as (4).

Rosette (10)—dark red.

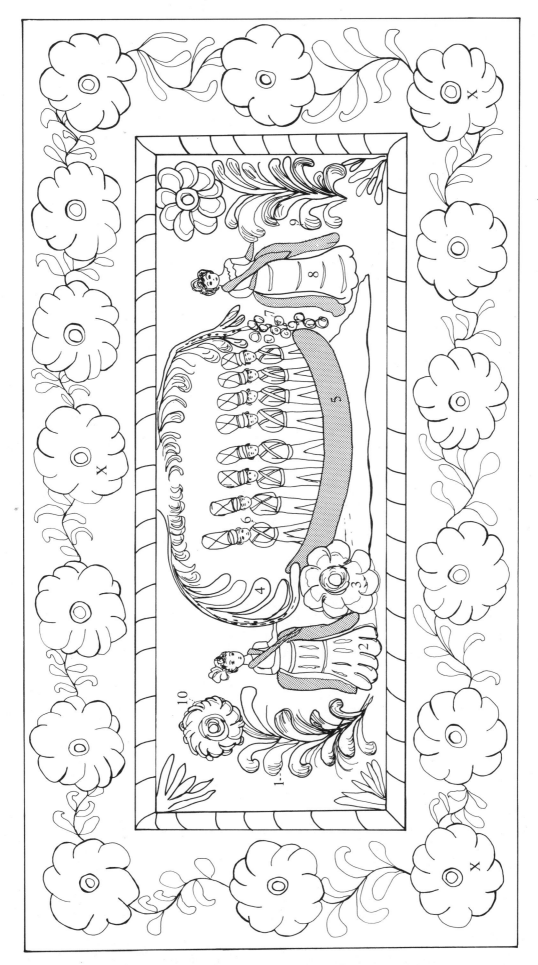

Chest Number 7, with two canoes and three soldiers in each, also from the Vierra collection, suggests a night scene on a lake. The stars sparkle here and there; birds of gorgeous plumage flit about, and the floral effects are tropical and exotic. The lakes about Mexico City might have suggested this scene to the artist.

Chest background—golden brown.

Border—black lines on dark blue.

Boat—brown edged in black.

Rosette—red edged in white.

Stars—black.

Water—white with black lines.

Leaves—alternating red and black, edges white.

Grapes—red with black centers.

Small circles—blue with black centers.

Men—coats black, hats black, plumes black.

Chest Number 8 is from the Spanish & Indian Trading Company. The rose red towers against a black background produce an outstanding contrast. On the platform or bridge stands a group of figures with high military hats, watching what suggests a sporting event. Two figures on white horses prance about in the foreground. The floral arrangement on all these chests, while having similar characteristics, shows distinctive style.

Rosette (1)—dark rose ground, yellow center, black ring around center.

Flower (2)—rose background, yellow leaves touched with white.

Narrow band connecting flowers—bright green dotted white; leaves on band—rose and green alternating.

Horse (3)—white; figure—hat red, coat and trousers blue; saddle—dark red.

Towers (4)—deep rose with shading in darker rose.

Figures on stand (5)—coats yellow, hats deep rose, plume black.

Pole (6)—yellow shaded white.

NEW ADAPTATIONS
FROM AUTHENTIC EXAMPLES
OF SPANISH COLONIAL FURNITURE

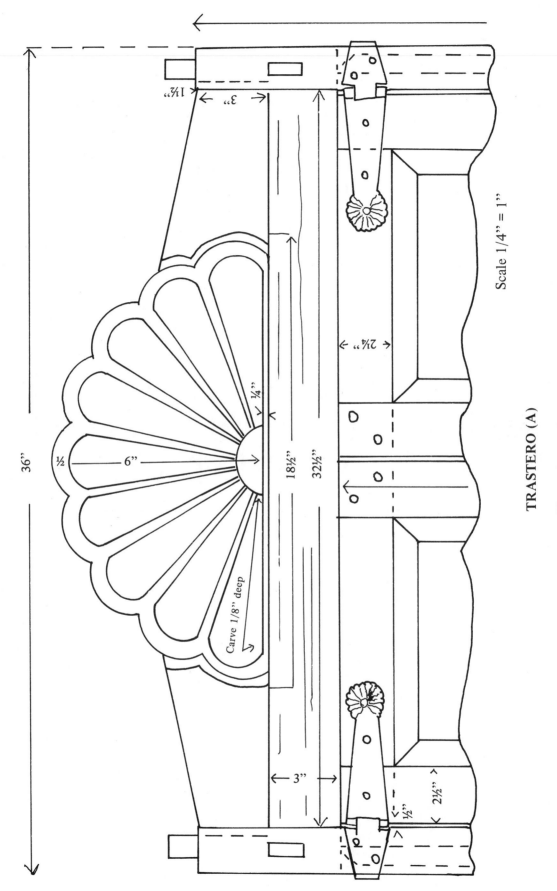

TRASTERO (A)

Upper front half

Scale 1/4" = 1"

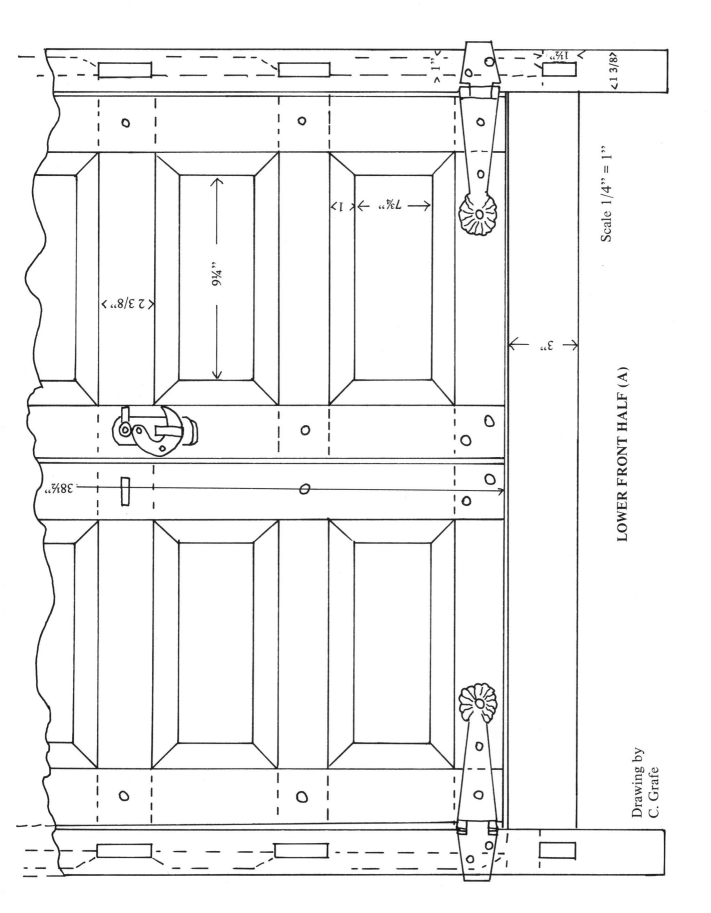

Scale 1/4" = 1"

LOWER FRONT HALF (A)

Drawing by
C. Grafe

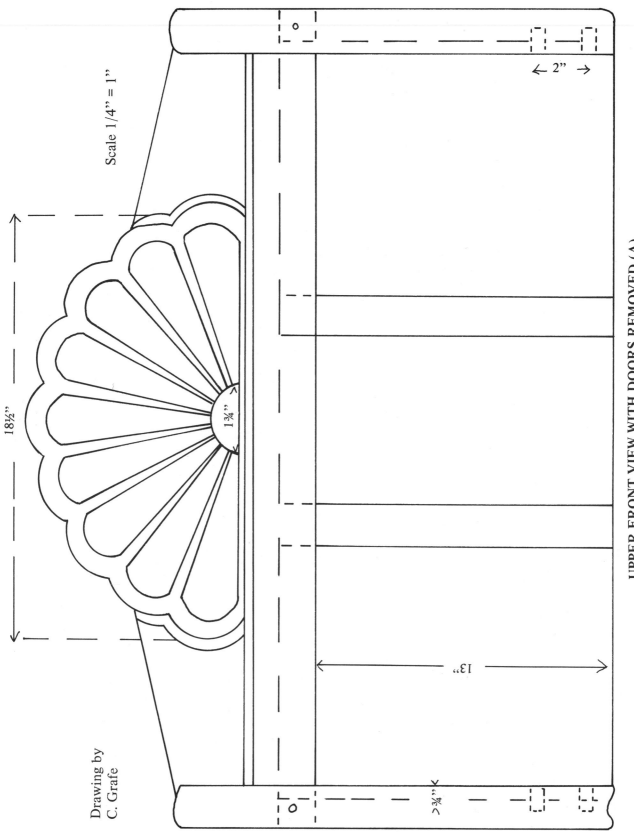

Scale 1/4" = 1"

18½"

1¾"

← 2" →

13"

¾"

Drawing by
C. Grafe

UPPER FRONT VIEW WITH DOORS REMOVED (A)

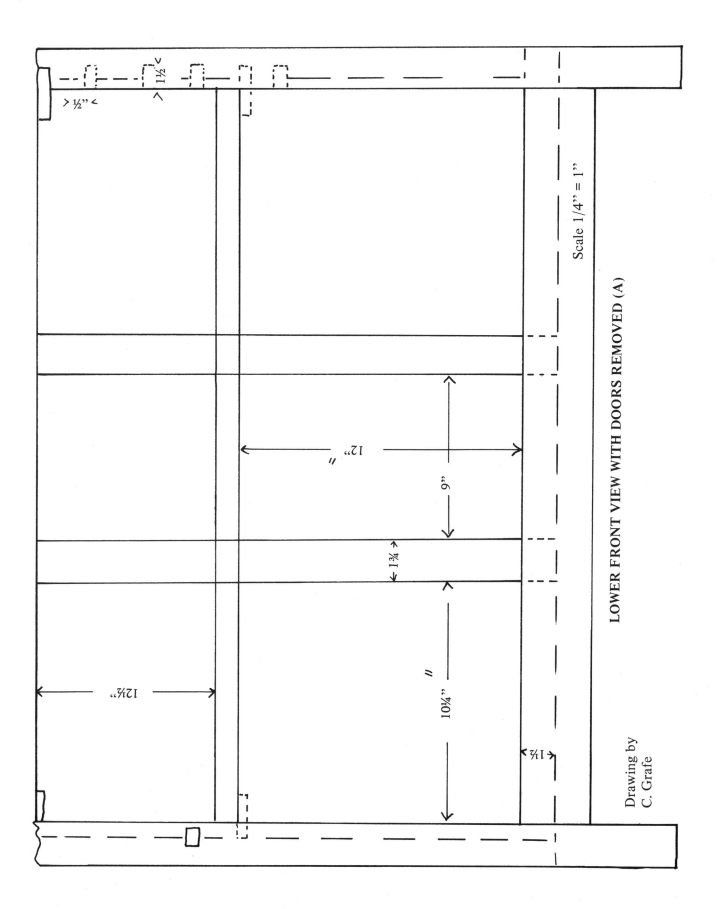

LOWER FRONT VIEW WITH DOORS REMOVED (A)

Scale 1/4" = 1"

Drawing by
C. Grafe

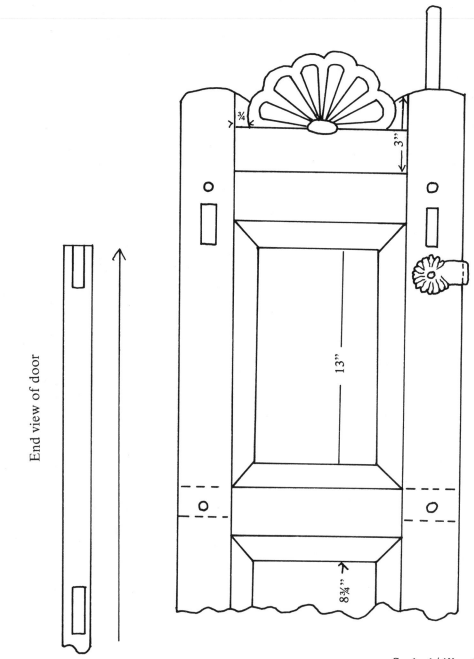

End view of door

¾

3"

13"

8¾"

Scale 1/4" = 1"

UPPER SIDE VIEW (A)

Drawing by
C. Grafe

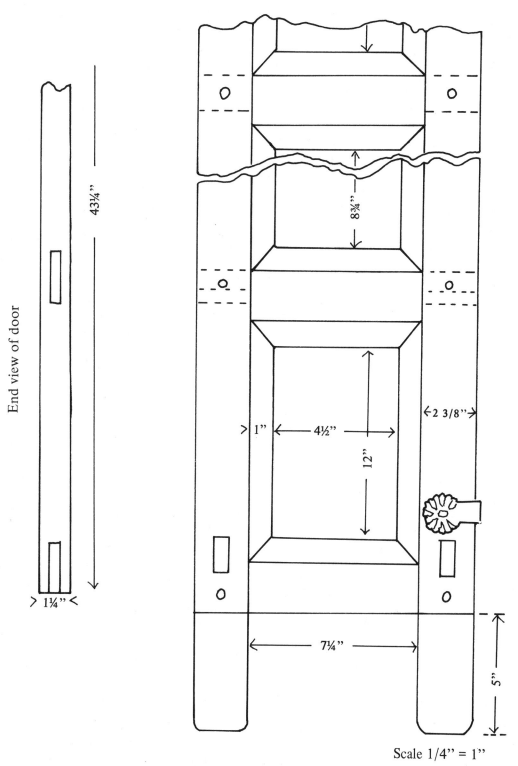

End view of door

43¼"

1¼"

8¾"

1"
4½"
12"
2 3/8"

7¼"

5"

Scale 1/4" = 1"

LOWER SIDE VIEW (A)

Drawing by
C. Grafe

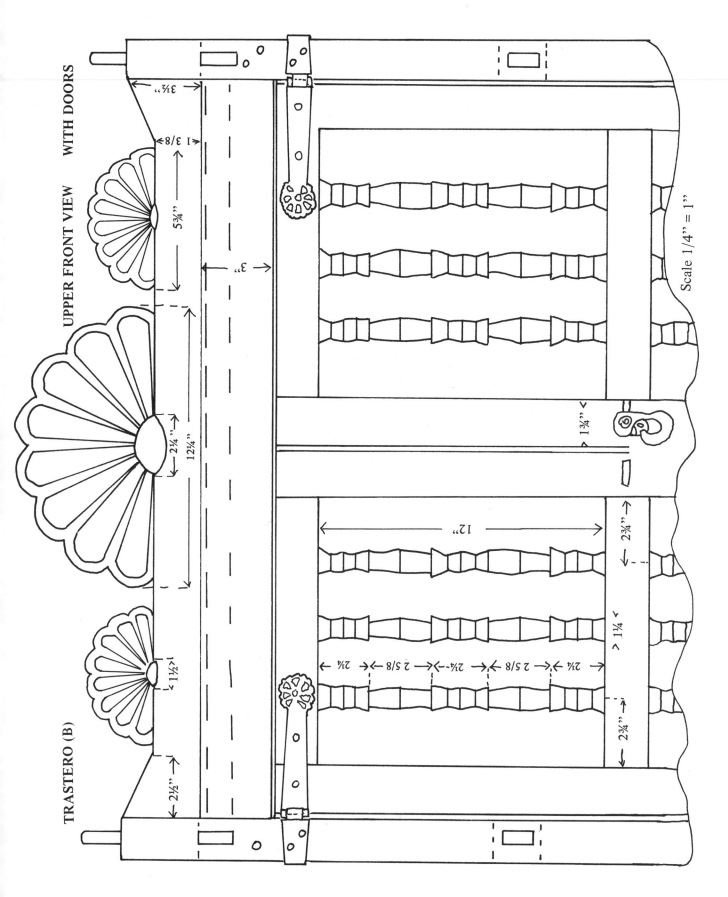

UPPER FRONT VIEW — WITH DOORS

TRASTERO (B)

Scale 1/4" = 1"

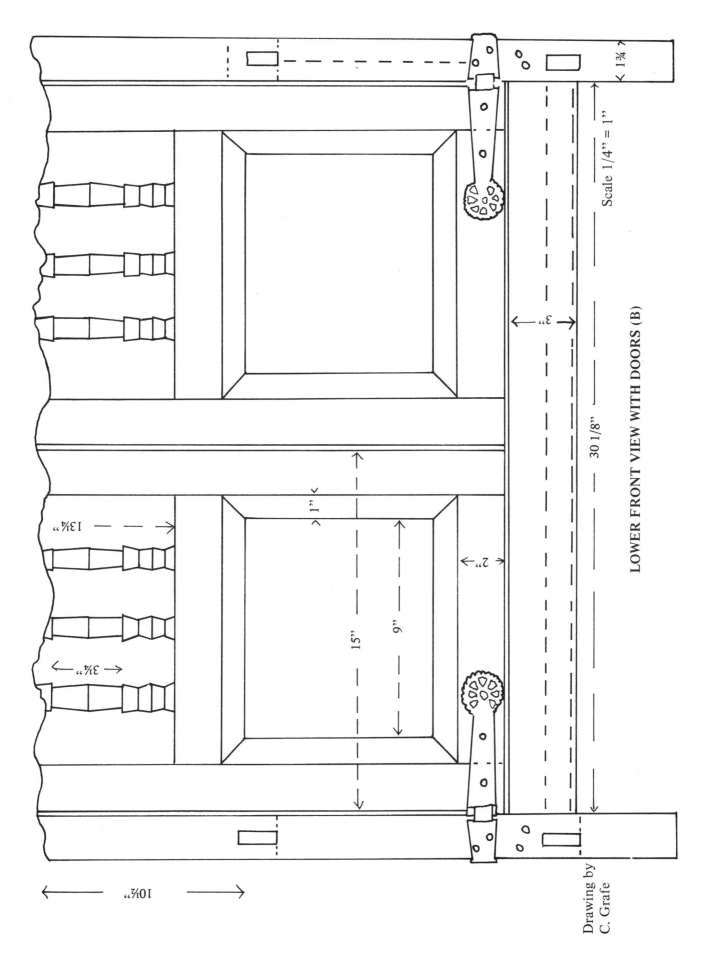

LOWER FRONT VIEW WITH DOORS (B)

Scale 1/4" = 1"

Drawing by
C. Grafe

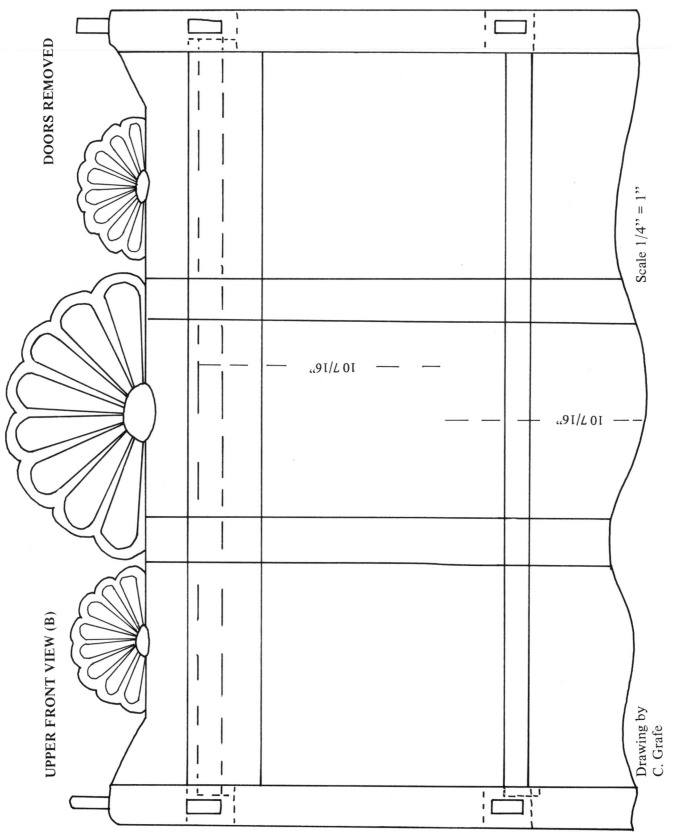

DOORS REMOVED

UPPER FRONT VIEW (B)

Scale 1/4" = 1"

10 7/16"

10 7/16"

Drawing by
C. Grafe

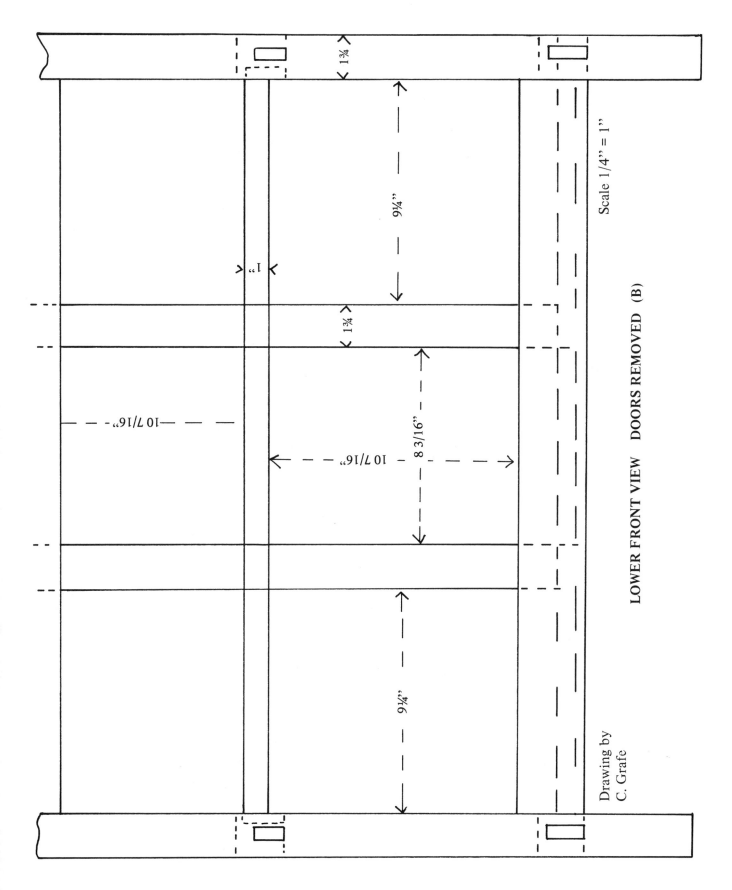

LOWER FRONT VIEW   DOORS REMOVED (B)

Scale 1/4" = 1"

Drawing by
C. Grafe

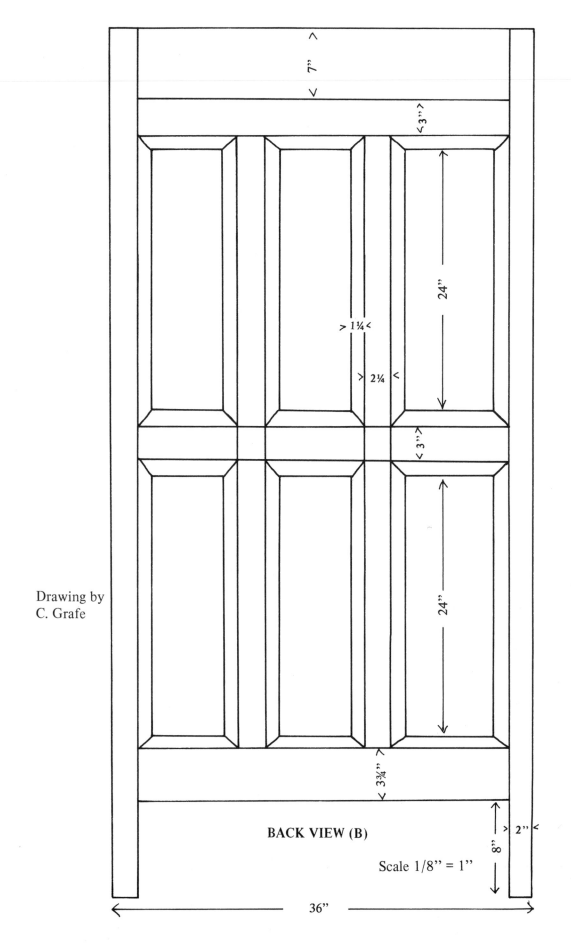

Drawing by
C. Grafe

BACK VIEW (B)

Scale 1/8" = 1"

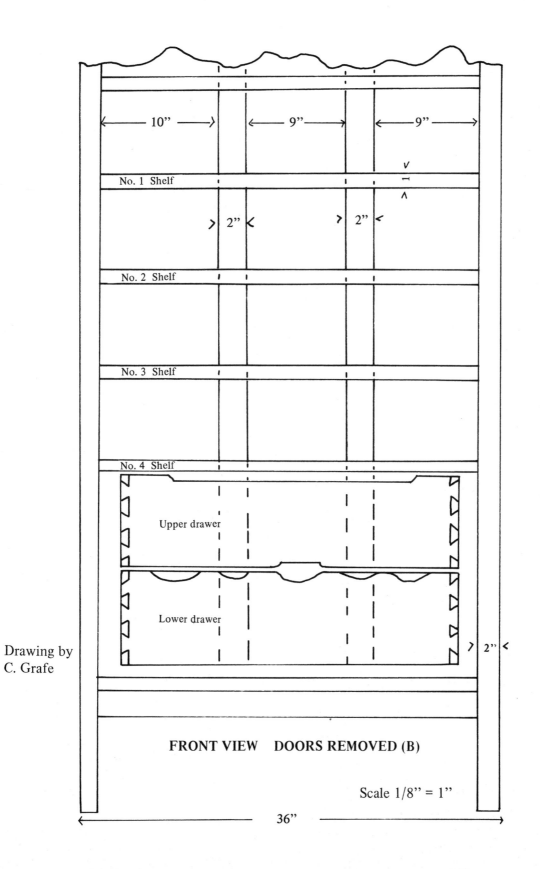

Drawing by
C. Grafe

FRONT VIEW   DOORS REMOVED (B)

Scale 1/8" = 1"

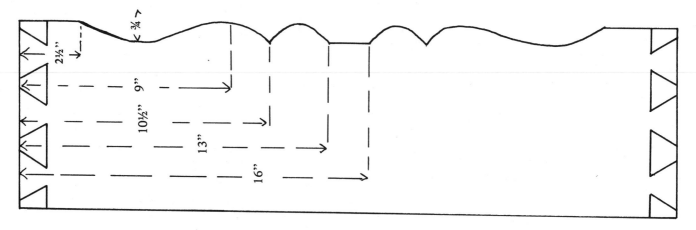

DETAILS OF LOWER DRAWER   FRONT VIEW (B)

End view same as upper drawer

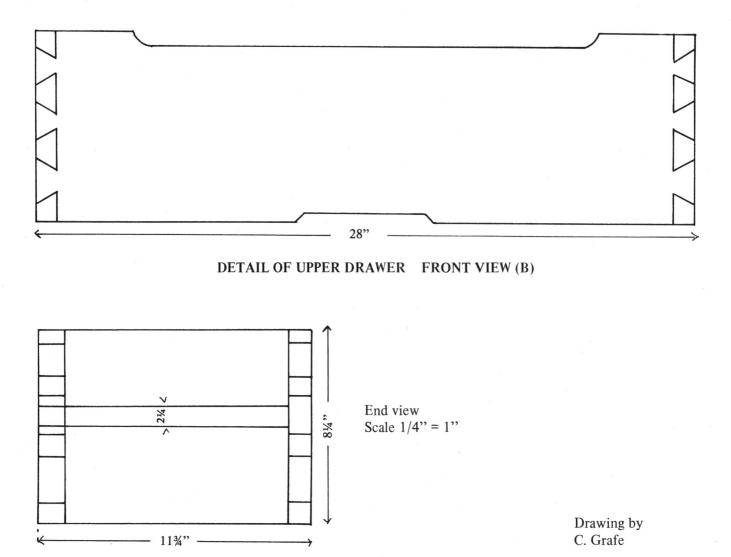

DETAIL OF UPPER DRAWER   FRONT VIEW (B)

End view
Scale 1/4" = 1"

Drawing by
C. Grafe

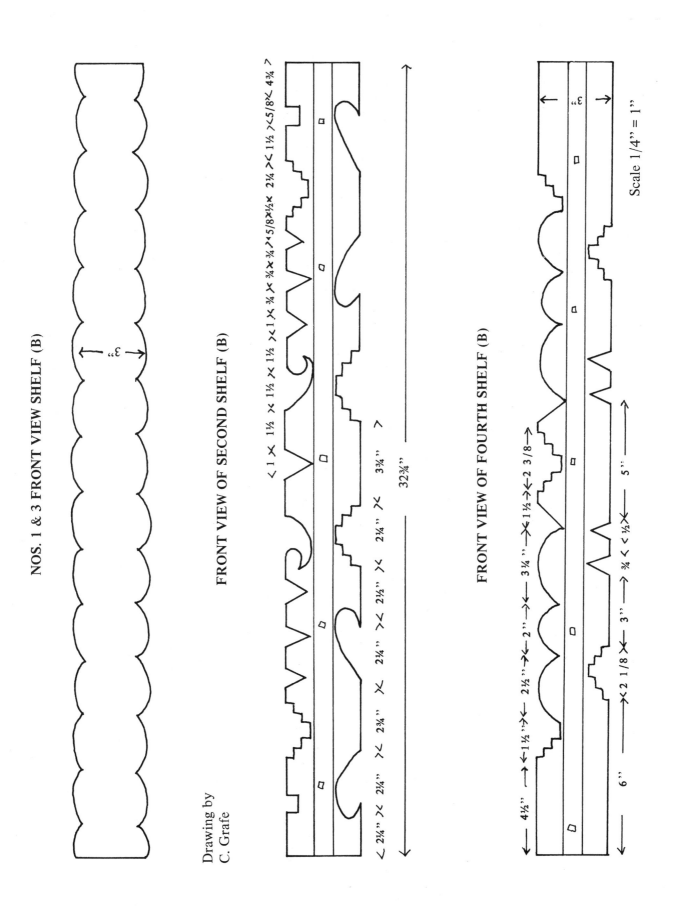

NOS. 1 & 3 FRONT VIEW SHELF (B)

3"

FRONT VIEW OF SECOND SHELF (B)

Drawing by
C. Grafe

< 1 × 1½ × 1½ ×< 1 × ¾ × ¾× ¾ ¾ > 5/8×½× 2¼ >< 1½ ><5/8>< 4¾ >

< 2¼" >< 2¼" >< 2¾" >< 2¼" >< 2½" >< 2¼" >< 3¾" >

32¾"

FRONT VIEW OF FOURTH SHELF (B)

< 4½" → ←1½"→← 2½" →←← 2" →← 3¼" →×← 1½ →←← 2 3/8 →

6" → ← 2 1/8 ×← 3" → ¾ < < ½ >< 5" →

3"

Scale 1/4" = 1"

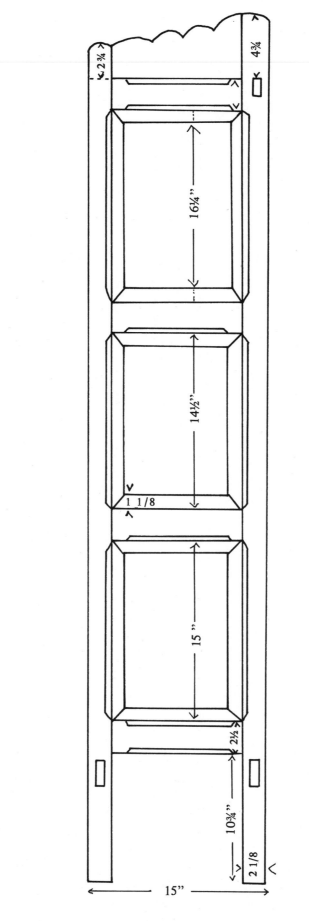

SIDE VIEW (B)

Scale 1/8" = 1"

Drawing by
C. Grafe

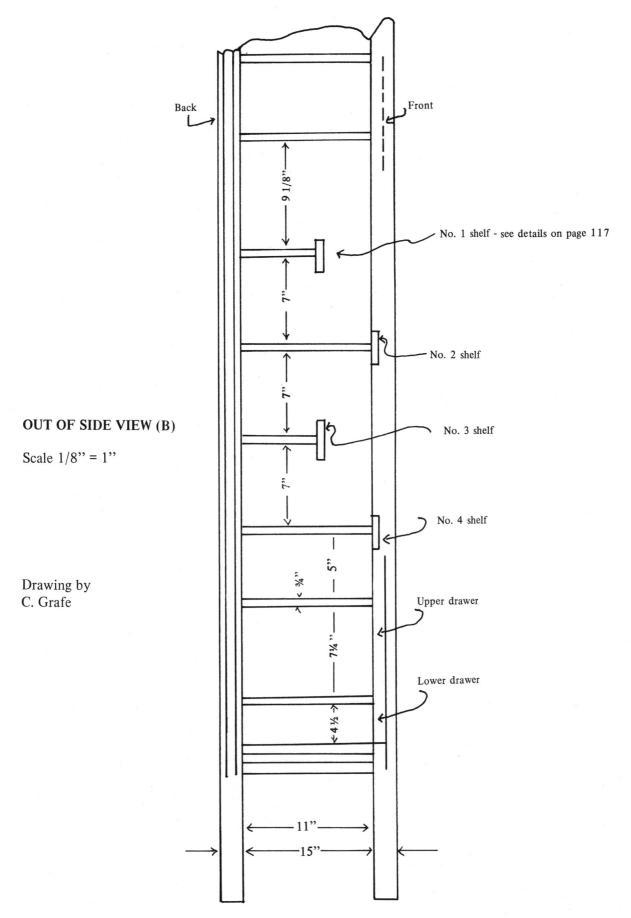

Back

Front

9 1/8"

No. 1 shelf - see details on page 117

7"

No. 2 shelf

OUT OF SIDE VIEW (B)

7"

Scale 1/8" = 1"

No. 3 shelf

7"

No. 4 shelf

Drawing by
C. Grafe

¾"

5"

Upper drawer

7¼"

Lower drawer

4½"

11"

15"

CHAIR   FRONT VIEW (A)

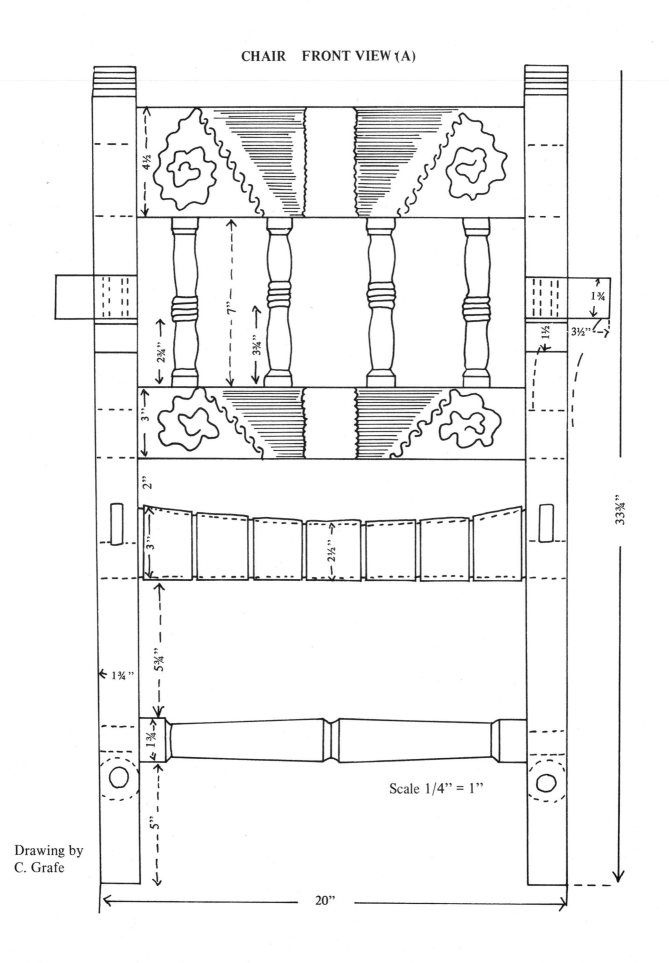

4½

7"

2¾"

3¾"

1¾

1½

3½"

3"

2"

3"

2½"

5¾"

1¾ "

1¾"

33¾"

5"

Scale 1/4" = 1"

Drawing by
C. Grafe

20"

CHAIR SIDE VIEW (A)

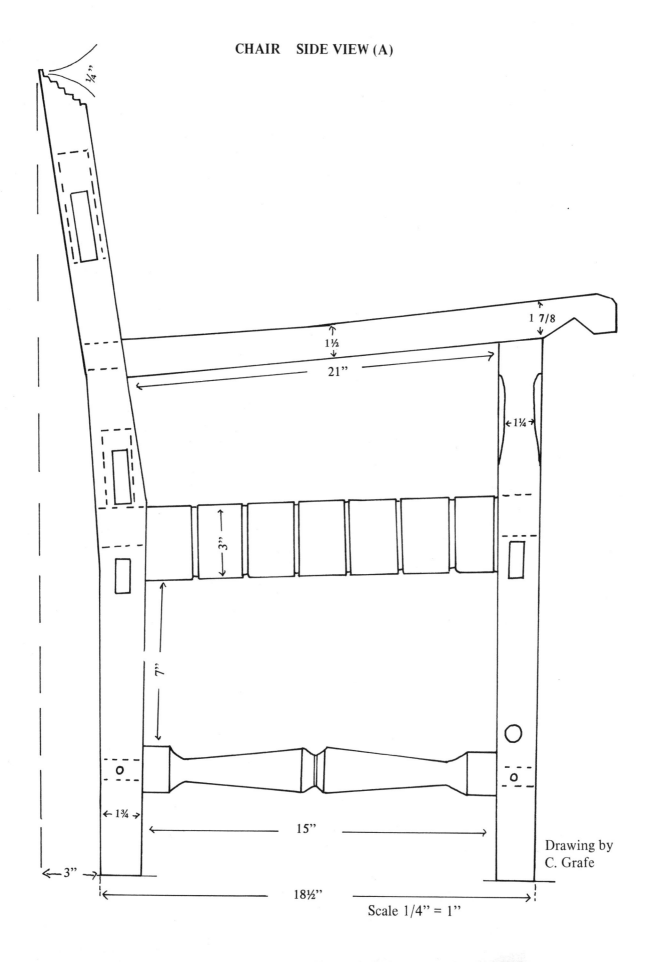

Drawing by
C. Grafe

Scale 1/4" = 1"

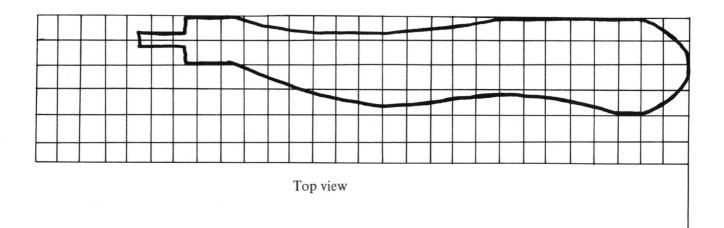

Top view

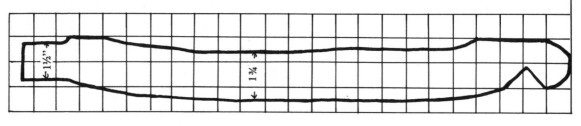

Side view

ARM REST DETAILS (A)

Scale 1/4" = 1"   1" squares

Drawing by
C. Grafe

CHAIR   FRONT VIEW (B)

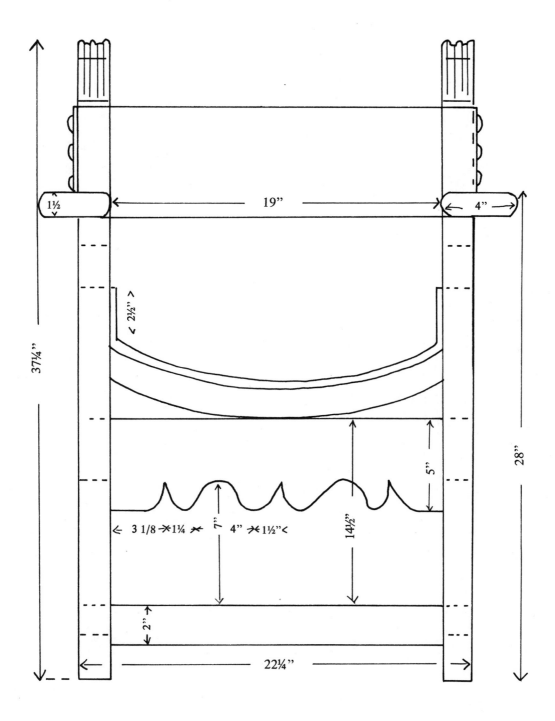

Scale 3/16" = 1"

Drawing by
C. Grafe

CHAIR   SIDE VIEW (B)

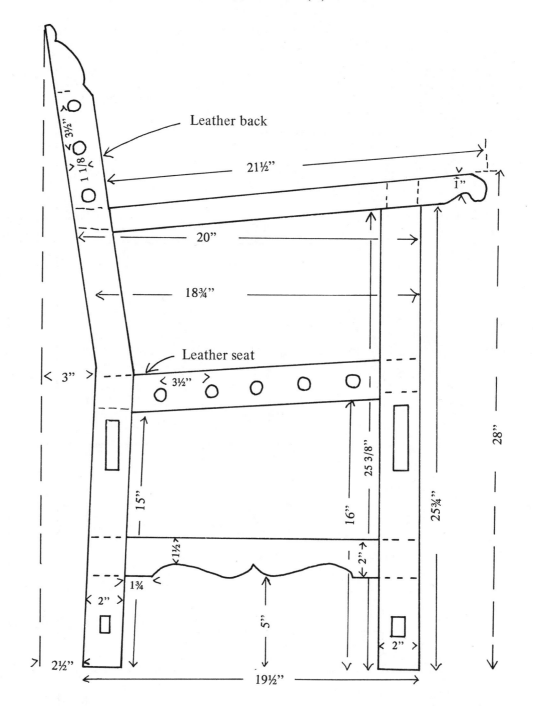

Leather back

21½"

1"

20"

18¾"

3½"

3½"

Leather seat

3"

25 3/8"

15"

16"

1½"

2"

1¾"

28"

25¾"

2"

5"

2"

2½"

2"

19½"

Scale 3/16" = 1"

Drawing by
C. Grafe

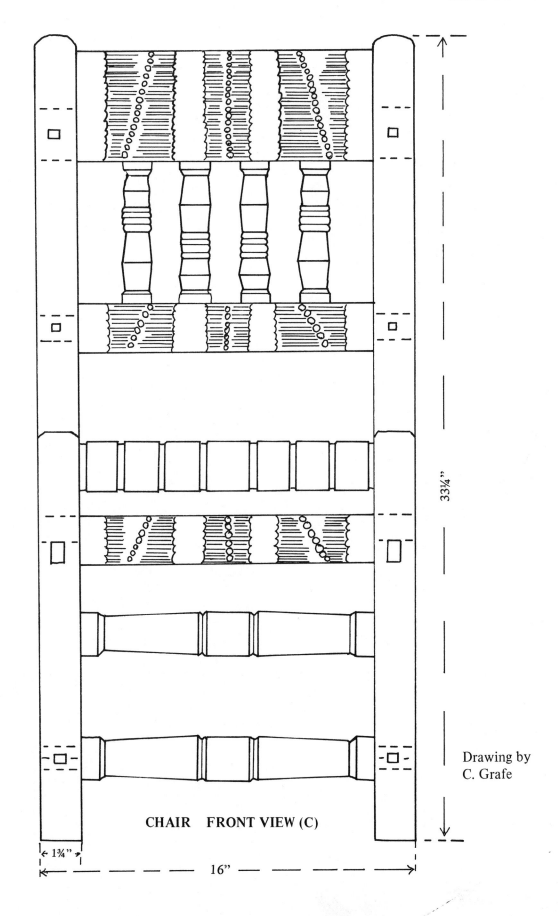

33¾"

Drawing by
C. Grafe

CHAIR   FRONT VIEW (C)

1¾"

16"

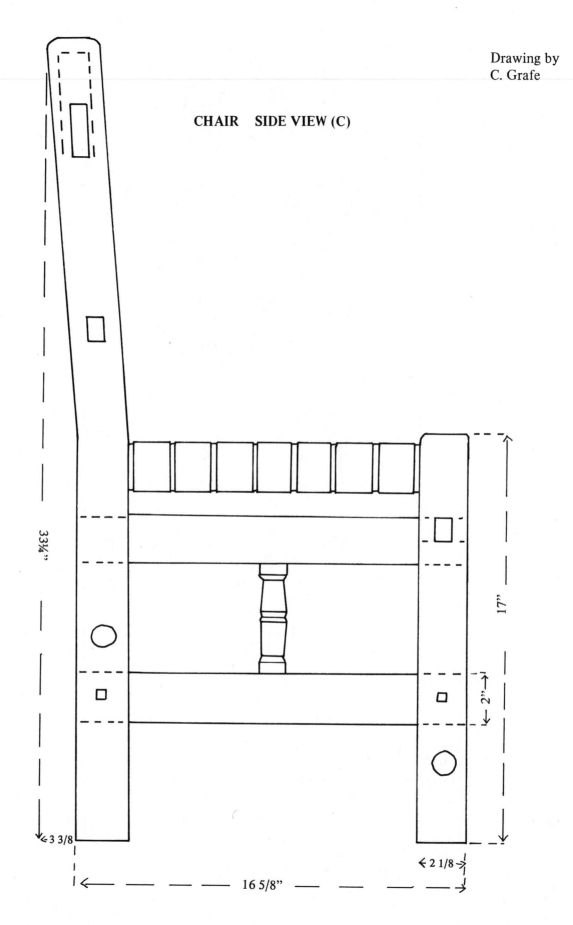

Drawing by
C. Grafe

CHAIR SIDE VIEW (C)

33¾"

17"

2"

← 3 3/8 →

← 2 1/8 →

← 16 5/8" →

Drawing by
C. Grafe

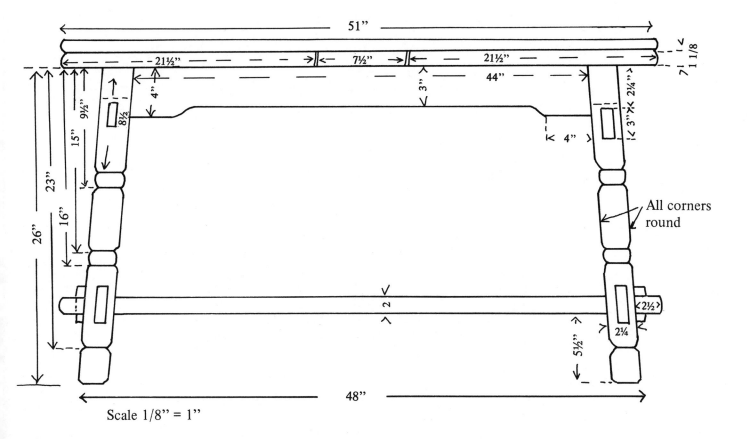

LONG FRONT VIEW OF DINING TABLE (A)

END VIEW OF DINING TABLE (A)

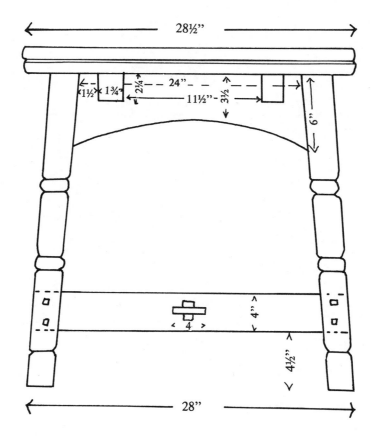

Scale 1/8" = 1"

Drawing by
C. Grafe

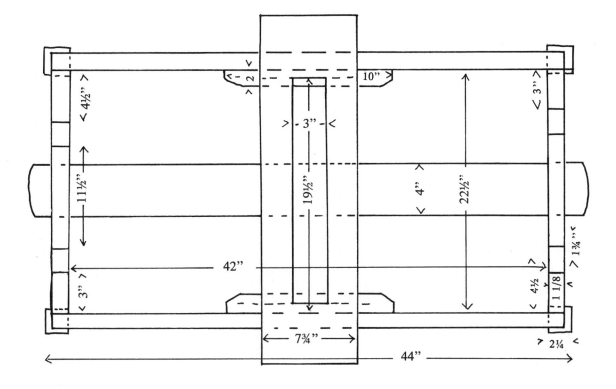

Scale 1/8" = 1"

Drawing by
C. Grafe

TOP VIEW OF TABLE FRAME (A)

Drawing by
C. Grafe

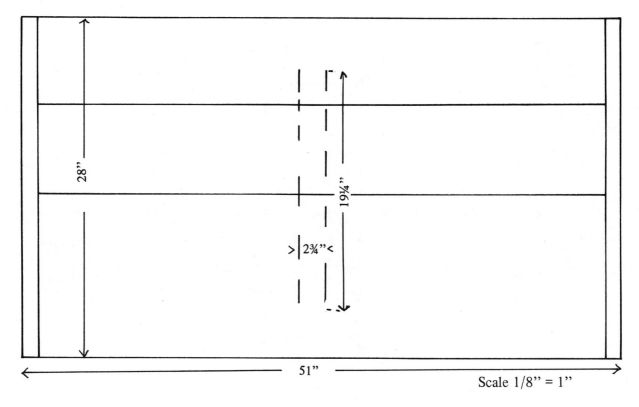

28"

19¼"

> 2¾" <

51"

Scale 1/8" = 1"

TOP VIEW OF MAIN TABLE LEAF (A)

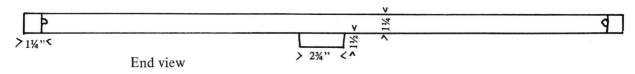

> 1¼" <

End view

> 2¾" <   1½   1¼

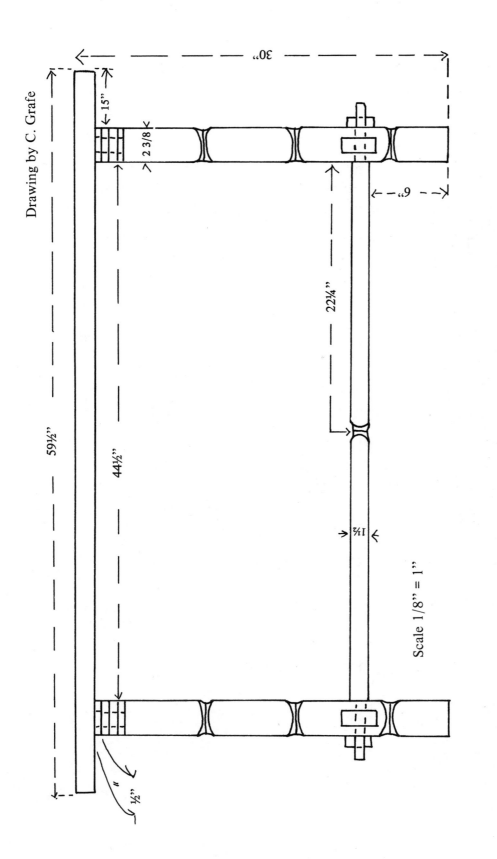

Drawing by C. Grafe

59½"

44½"

15"

2 3/8

30"

22¼"

6"

1½

½"

Scale 1/8" = 1"

TABLE   FRONT VIEW (B)

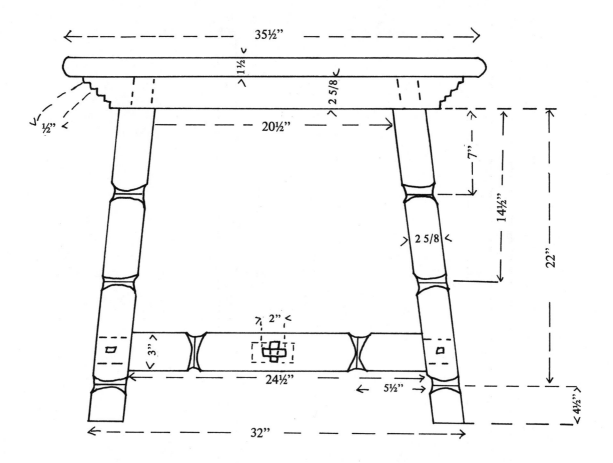

Scale 1/8" = 1"

Drawing by
C. Grafe

TABLE   END VIEW (B)

Books of Related Interest
from Ancient City Press

THE ADOBE BOOK, by John F. O'Connor. 1973.
Detailed how-to covering every phase of construction.

ECHOES OF THE FLUTE, by Lorenzo de Córdova. 1972 (2d printing 1982).
Old Hispanic village Lenten, funeral and Penitente Brotherhood customs in northern New Mexico.

THE GENUINE NEW MEXICO TASTY RECIPES,
by Cleofas M. Jaramillo. 1981.
Reprint of rare 1942 cookbook with seventy-five delicious old-time New Mexican Spanish recipes and additional materials on traditional Hispano food.

HISPANIC ARTS AND ETHNOHISTORY IN THE SOUTHWEST:
New Papers Inspired by the Work of E. Boyd,
edited by Marta Weigle with Claudia Larcombe
and Samuel Larcombe. 1983.
Twenty-two articles by twenty-three scholars, including Marc Simmons, on traditional Hispanic arts, their preservation, and 17-19th-century life in New Mexico. A Spanish Colonial Arts Society book published by Ancient City Press and the University of New Mexico Press.

NEW MEXICO ARTISTS AND WRITERS: A Celebration, 1940,
edited and compiled by Marta Weigle and Kyle Fiore. 1982.
Oversized newspaper with facsimile reprint of June 26, 1940, special 38-page edition of *The Santa Fe New Mexican,* "Prominent Artists and Writers of New Mexico," with additional contemporaneous materials.

THE PENITENTES OF THE SOUTHWEST, by Marta Weigle.
1970 (3d printing 1982).
History and description of Brotherhood organization, rites and arts.

SANTA FE AND TAOS: The Writer's Era, 1916-1941,
by Marta Weigle and Kyle Fiore. 1982.
Writers', publishers' and printers' civic and literary activities chronicled and illustrated; articles by D. H. Lawrence, Mabel Dodge Luhan, Ruth Laughlin and Elizabeth Shepley Sergeant.

SANTOS AND SAINTS: The Religious Folk Art of Hispanic New Mexico,
by Thomas J. Steele, S. J. Reprint of 1974 ed. with 1982 update.
Historical, sociological and theological analysis of Hispanic folk art and religion in New Mexico.

EL SANTUARIO DE CHIMAYO, by Stephen F. de Borhegyi and E. Boyd. 1956 (1982 printing).
History and detailed description of the famous healing shrine north of Santa Fe. A Spanish Colonial Arts Society book.

SHADOWS OF THE PAST, by Cleofas M. Jaramillo. 1980 reprint of the 1941 Seton Village Press ed.
Family history and firsthand account of Hispanic folklore and customs in 19th-century northern New Mexico.